PLANT-POWERED PROTEIN

ALSO BY NAVA ATLAS

COOKBOOKS

Vegan on a Budget

5-Ingredient Vegan

Plant Power

Wild About Greens

Vegan Holiday Kitchen

Vegan Soups and Hearty Stews for All Seasons

Vegan Express

The Vegetarian Family Cookbook

The Vegetarian 5-Ingredient Gourmet

Great American Vegetarian

Vegetarian Express

Vegetarian Celebrations

Vegetariana

VISUAL NONFICTION

The Literary Ladies' Guide to the Writing Life

Secret Recipes for the Modern Wife

Expect the Unexpected When You're Expecting! (A Parody)

PLANT-POWERED PROTEIN

125 RECIPES FOR USING TODAY'S AMAZING MEAT ALTERNATIVES

NAVA ATLAS

PHOTOGRAPHS BY HANNAH KAMINSKY

GRAND CENTRAL PUBLISHING

NEW YORK BOSTON

Grand Central Publishing
Hachette Book Group
1290 Avenue of the Americas,
New York, NY 10104

grandcentralpublishing.com

twitter.com/grandcentralpub

First Edition: December 2020

Grand Central Publishing is a division of Hachette Book Group, Inc. The Grand Central Publishing name and logo is a trademark of Hachette Book Group, Inc.

The publisher is not responsible for websites (or their content) that are not owned by the publisher.

The Hachette Speakers Bureau provides a wide range of authors for speaking events. To find out more, go to www.hachettespeakersbureau.com or call (866) 376-6591.

Library of Congress Cataloging-in-Publication Data.

Names: Atlas, Nava, author. | Kaminsky, Hannah, 1989- photographer.
Title: Plant-powered protein : 125 recipes for using today's amazing meat alternatives / Nava Atlas ; photographs by Hannah Kaminsky.
Description: New York : Grand Central Publishing, 2020. | Includes index. | Identifiers: LCCN 2020022708 | ISBN 9781538718735 (hardcover) | ISBN 9781538718728 (ebook)
Subjects: LCSH: Meat substitutes. | Vegan cooking. | LCGFT: Cookbooks.
Classification: LCC TX838 .A85 2020 | DDC 641.5/6362—dc23
LC record available at https://lccn.loc.gov/2020022708

ISBNs: 978-1-5387-1873-5 (hardcover); 978-1-5387-1872-8 (ebook)

Printed in China

APS

10 9 8 7 6 5 4 3 2 1

CONTENTS

INTRODUCTION

Whether you're a veg-curious omnivore, a vegetarian wanting to take the final steps toward veganism, or a seasoned vegan looking for ways to shake up your meal rotation, **welcome to the plant-powered protein revolution!**

There are lots of compelling reasons to rethink our relationship with protein, and fortunately, that's easier (and more delicious) to do than ever before. In the pages ahead, you'll discover new ways to prepare familiar favorites, from nostalgic comfort classics to bold global fare, that are kinder to the earth and better for your health than animal-based proteins. Most of the recipes in this book are easy enough for weeknight meals and flavorful enough to satisfy even the pickiest of eaters. The plant-based meat industry is rapidly changing, and I'm excited to be part of the revolution.

I'm one of those vegans who's been known to claim that I'm not a big fan of meat-like flavors and textures. I gave up meat eons ago, mainly because I didn't like the bland, flavorless dishes my mom (may she rest in peace) made and served. I *wanted* more vegetables—preferably not overcooked! It was only later, when information on animal agriculture became readily available, that I transitioned from rebellious vegetarian to ethical vegan—for the animals, mostly, but also because of the environmental damage caused by animal agriculture.

That said, I've never had an argument with meat alternatives: though I more often gravitate to beans and tofu, I've never made a point of avoiding them. I've always enjoyed vegan burgers, for example, because in days gone by (less so today) they were often the only plant-based option on restaurant menus. I don't compare them to the last beef burger I had decades ago; they're often good in their own right, whether based on black beans or pea protein.

Pulled-Protein Tacos with
Fruity Corn-Pineapple
Salsa, page 151

Page 165

ABOUT THE RECIPES— SOMETHING FOR EVERYONE

The recipes in this book feature beefy crumbles, deli slices, chicken-style chunks and strips, vegan sausage, and lots more—even a brief introduction to plant-based seafood. Many plant meats are either ready to use or nearly ready, so why do we need recipes for using them at all? Why not open *The Joy of Cooking*, for example, and swap plant protein for animal meats? (Feel free to do just that; it sounds like fun!)

The answer is that it's not just about simply swapping plant-based grounds for ground beef, for example. These recipes present an opportunity to use plant-based products thoughtfully in dishes that contain other wholesome ingredients and lots of fresh vegetables—bridging the divide between traditional American comfort food and plant-based whole foods.

In addition, there are plenty of cookbooks, obviously, that use actual meat in recipes, along with carefully chosen ingredients and flavorings that will produce the best results. Using plant-based meats requires a similar approach. To that end, these recipes will explore ways to tease out the best flavors and most appealing uses for meat alternatives.

Some plant-based meats are already nicely flavored straight out of the package (one example of this is plant-based sausages, such as plant-based chorizo); others are bland but offer meaty textures. In some cases, otherwise good products are high in sodium. Creating recipes with lots of healthful ingredients will mitigate sodium content by dispersing it throughout a dish filled with vegetables, grains, pasta, beans, nuts, and/or seeds.

One of the things I learned at 2019's Plant-Based World Conference and Expo is that many producers of plant proteins are looking to improve the nutritional profile of their products. The aim is

The truth is that I've been making "meaty" things even while professing not to. I've schlepped various iterations of mock chicken noodle soup from one book to another (including this one—how could I leave it out?). I'm also such a big fan of seitan that I make my own, and that's a food that's nothing if not meaty. One of my most famous recipes, and the one I probably make most often, is the one for "tofuna," a ridiculously easy concoction of baked tofu, vegan mayo, and celery. Whenever I serve this, people are completely aware that it's faux—and it practically gets inhaled anyway. I'm tickled that one of my nonvegan neighbors has adopted it as his go-to portable work lunch, preferring it to real tuna or chicken.

Rather amusingly, my grown son and daughter, lifelong vegetarians and now longtime vegans, have always loved meat alternatives—even though they've never tasted the real thing! There's unquestionably something about meaty flavors and textures that has a primal appeal, speaking to a universal craving for a certain kind of umami.

to achieve more flavor and better texture with less sodium. Not all plant proteins are created equal when it comes to sodium, though. Some, such as plain pea-protein crumbles and Soy Curls, have no sodium at all—they're a blank canvas for your own seasonings. The same is true of two traditional plant proteins, tofu and tempeh.

Just as protein can be considered the building block of a sound diet, vegetables, grains, beans, nuts, and seeds form the foundation of protein. Most of the recipes in this collection offer several options for plant protein. For whole-foods fans, you'll find recipes using tofu, tempeh, and/or seitan. Those with a DIY spirit may enjoy making their own plant-based meat substitutes from scratch with ingredients such as gluten flour (also known as vital wheat gluten), quinoa, nuts, beans, and tempeh. You'll find those kinds of recipes in chapter 9 (page 213). The recipes also take a cue from global cuisines in that they use protein as a modest part of a dish rather than its central focus.

THE PLANT-BASED PROTEIN MOVEMENT

Beyond Meat's groundbreaking 2019 initial public offering helped raise consumer awareness of plant-based proteins. Suddenly it seemed that plant meats were everywhere, and buzz has been building ever since. Of course, their appearance really wasn't all that sudden. While Beyond Meat and Impossible products have done much to increase their visibility, meat analogs are nothing new. They've been a part of Asian cuisines for centuries, for example. Now there's a major shift in how "meat" is defined.

What ultimately persuaded me to pursue a book on this topic was a *New York Times* article profiling Bruce Friedrich, formerly of PETA, who famously threw fake blood at models wearing furs at fashion shows. The article's title proclaimed: "This Animal Activist Used to Get in Your Face. Now He's Going After Your Palate." Friedrich realized that the guilt approach wasn't working. In 2015 he founded the Good Food Institute with a new goal: to reach meat eaters with plant-based meat alternatives. And if the result would be a healthier planet and fewer animals being harmed, that's what mattered.

According to the article, Friedrich "came to realize that making others feel bad about eating meat does not make them consume less of it." Much of his new approach has involved lobbying, research, and corporate engagement. And it seems to be working—the rapid development of plant-based protein companies and the explosive growth of meat alternatives are proof positive.

With lots of passion (as well as profit) driving this growth, it's a trend, like veganism itself, that looks like it's here to stay. Indeed, *The Economist* proclaimed 2019 "The Year of the Vegan": "Where millennials lead, businesses and governments will follow." While it's risky to paint any generation with a broad brush, millennials and those who have come after them are the driving force behind the global movement toward reducing the consumption of meat. Thank you, millennials!

The article goes on to state: "The business of providing vegan meals is booming.... Sales of vegan foods in America in the year to June 2018 rose ten times faster than food sales as a whole. Giant food firms are clambering onto the bandwagon, creating vegan lines of their own, buying startups, or both.... Even Big Meat is going vegan, it seems."

Plant proteins are quickly taking their place in food service and restaurants, but home cooks also have a growing array of options. Today's vegan chefs and activists appreciate the idea that plant meats can be a bridge for omnivores who might otherwise be resistant to vegan fare.

Barbecue Beefy Tacos, page 148

Now the entire concept of meat is being redefined. Companies involved are changing the language as well by not using the terms "meat alternatives" or "faux meats" but rather "plant protein," "plant-based protein," and simply "plant meat." Even some actual meat companies are joining the movement rather than fighting it (though some are, indeed, fighting it).

Moving toward a plant-based paradigm is also smart from an economic perspective. Plant protein is significantly cheaper to produce and distribute than animal meats. Today, 41 percent of America's landmass is given over to cattle grazing. That's the very definition of inefficiency. Quoting *The Economist*: "If plant-based 'meats' take off, they could become a transformative technology, improving Westerners' protein-heavy diets, reducing the environmental hoofprint of animal husbandry and perhaps even cutting the cost of food in poor countries."

In just a short span of time, plant-based meat alternatives that didn't exist not so long ago are already staples in restaurant chains and supermarkets—not just in the natural foods aisle but also in the meat department. For anyone who wants to explore a plant-based diet, there's no sacrifice whatsoever now that we have fantastic animal-free stand-ins for nearly every kind of meat, seafood, and dairy product.

ENVIRONMENTAL CONCERNS AND CLIMATE CHANGE

This is a cookbook, not a treatise on climate change, but I'd be remiss if I didn't mention that one of the forces behind the plant-protein movement is the desire to mitigate the climate crisis.

Whether made from pea protein, non-GMO soy, or other plants, a serving of plant protein uses 99 percent less water and 93 percent less land than animal protein. So while governments continue to waffle about protecting the environment and animals, socially responsible entrepreneurs and investors are taking control of the narrative and driving the change. When I give talks, I like to remind people that reducing or eliminating animals from their diets is something positive that they can do every day.

We need no further proof of climate change than the calamitous events that happen regularly, but the contributions made by animal agriculture to our warming planet should be a greater part of the conversation. Alon Shepon of the T. H. Chan School of Public Health (Harvard University) has made the case for a plant-based diet to help alleviate the climate crisis: "By 2050 greenhouse emissions from agriculture in a vegan world would be 70 percent lower than in a world where people ate as they do today."

A groundbreaking 2006 report by the Food and Agriculture Organization of the United Nations is still relevant and often cited. According to this report, the animal agriculture sector accounts for 18 percent of global human-induced greenhouse gas emissions. Further, it states that "mapping has shown a strong relationship between excessive nitrogen in the atmosphere and the location of intensive farm animal production areas." Deforestation for farm-animal grazing has devastating repercussions for the environment as well, with thousands of acres of rain forest and other lands still being cleared yearly for cattle grazing.

Animal agriculture has little to recommend it. There's the insane use of water, the pollution of air and streams, and the overuse of pesticides and antibiotics. So many of these issues can be alleviated by changing our protein source to plants.

COMPASSION FOR ANIMALS

For ethical vegans, the driving motivation is all about compassion for sentient beings. Those who choose to go vegan appreciate knowing that their food choices are not only tasty and healthful but also humane.

I can't tell you how many people I've heard say something like, "I can't look at what happens to animals, because if I did, I wouldn't be able to eat meat." Often, it's not that people don't know; they just don't want to look. But putting on emotional blinders doesn't mean that the inhumane and unsustainable treatment of animals isn't happening.

I've also heard people say, "Why should I eat a fake burger? If I want to eat a burger once in a while, I'll eat the real thing." This not only ignores the facts on the ground for animals; it also ignores the environmental reality.

I'll keep this part brief but will end with a plea: do the research and open your heart!

THE PROTEIN QUESTION

If you've gone plant-based, or are going in that direction, you'll inevitably be asked, "How do you get your protein?" It's a question that just won't go away. It's not at all complicated; plant-based protein sources are abundant, and I'll explore them here.

Longtime vegans tend to roll their eyes at having to explain and justify their protein sources. But the myth that it's hard to get adequate protein on a vegan diet is tenacious, so it's better to address it than to ignore it. I find that people ask me this question not because they're challenging me but because they want to learn.

Reed Mangels, RD, PhD, the nutrition adviser to the Vegetarian Resource Group, concurs. On VRG's website, she states: "Vegans are bombarded with questions about where they get their protein.... This concern about protein is misplaced. Although protein is certainly an essential nutrient which plays many key roles in the way our bodies function, we do not need huge quantities of it. Only about one calorie out of every 10 we take in needs to come from protein."

There's plenty of evidence that a varied whole-foods diet has little chance of falling short in protein, especially if it provides sufficient calories. Many foods have at least some protein. Whole grains, legumes, soy foods, nuts, and seeds all offer high-quality protein. Lots of common vegetables have small amounts of protein, so if you eat plenty of them, they add to your daily intake as well.

The body can manufacture all but nine of the twenty-two amino acids that make up proteins. These nine amino acids are referred to as essential amino acids and must be gotten from food. That is why getting sufficient good-quality protein is crucial. The operative word here is "sufficient"—this isn't a case where more is necessarily better. Many Americans eat twice as much protein as they need. Excess protein can't be stored, and its elimination puts a strain on the body's organs and functions.

Figuring out how much protein you need is based on a simple calculation. The recommended daily allowance (RDA) established by the National Academy of Sciences states that an adult in good health needs 0.36 grams of protein per pound of body weight per day. So a 160-pound man needs around 58 grams of protein a day, and a 120-pound woman needs around 43 grams.

There are exceptions to the RDAs: pregnant and lactating woman need considerably more protein—add at least 25 grams of protein per day. Infants and children need more total protein per pound of body weight than adults. Athletes need a lot more protein, but its preferred source, once thought to be animal products, is shifting to plants. Many well-known athletes, including those considered elite or superathletes, have gone vegan. *The Game Changers,* a 2019 film, explores this trend with many amazing examples. If you have specific questions about your own protein needs, I suggest talking to a registered dietitian.

PROTEIN QUANTITIES IN PLANT-BASED FOODS

Because the underlying theme of this book is plant protein, let's take a look at some common sources of it in addition to the meaty, ready-made plant-based proteins that star in this book's recipes. The amount of protein is given in grams.

Beans and Legumes (Cooked, ½-Cup Serving)

Beans and legumes are low in calories and fat, so if you need to consume more protein, a 1-cup serving—double the amount below—is completely reasonable.

Lentils, red = 13g
Split peas, green or yellow = 8–10g
Black beans = 8g
Chickpeas = 7g
Lentils, brown = 6–8g
Pinto beans = 6g

Tofu, Tempeh, and Seitan

The original plant-based protein trio will be making regular appearances throughout the following chapters.

Seitan (4 ounces) = 28g
Tempeh (4 ounces) = 20–21g
Tofu, baked (2 ounces) = 11g
Tofu, firm (4 ounces) = 10g
Tofu, extra-firm (4 ounces) = 8g

Page 45

Grains (Cooked, ½-Cup Serving)

Like legumes, whole grains are low in fat and high in fiber. A 1-cup serving for people with hearty appetites or high protein needs is a reasonable quantity.

Barley = 8g

Oats, steel-cut = 5g

Oats, old-fashioned = 5g

Quinoa = 4–4.5g

Rice, brown = 3g

Nutritional Yeast

The protein content of nutritional yeast varies; the amount below applies to the Red Star brand. Nutritional yeast is also a great source of vitamin B_{12}—one serving gives you 130 percent of your RDA.

1½ tablespoons = 8g

Pasta (Cooked, 1-Cup Serving)

Spelt pasta = 12g

Soba noodles (2-ounce serving) = 7–8g

Whole wheat pasta = 7g

Durum wheat pasta = 7g

Quinoa pasta = 4g

Vegetables

Asparagus (1 cup chopped) = 4g

Brussels sprouts (1 cup) = 4g

Spinach (wilted and packed, ½ cup) = 3g

Broccoli (1 cup florets) = 2–3g

Sweet potato (1 medium) = 2.25g

Kale (chopped and packed, 1 cup) = 2g

Nuts (¼-Cup Serving)

Almonds = 8g

Peanuts = 7g

Pistachios = 6g

Cashews = 5g

Walnuts = 4g

Nut Butters (2-Tablespoon Serving)

Peanut butter = 8g

Almond butter = 8g

Cashew butter = 6g

Seeds (1-Ounce Serving)

Pumpkin seeds = 7g

Hemp seeds = 6g

Sesame seeds = 6g

Flaxseeds = 5g

Chia seeds = 4.7g

Sunflower seeds = 3.5g

Page 53

Dr. Praeger's Classic Chick'n Tenders (3 pieces) = 14g

Good Catch Fish-Free Tuna (3.3-ounce serving) = 14g

Gardein Beefless Ground (½ cup) = 12g

Lightlife Smoky Tempeh Strips (4 strips) = 12g

Yves Veggie Cuisine Veggie Ham (5 slices) = 12g

SoyBoy Not Dogs (2-link serving) = 11g

MOVING TOWARD A PLANT-BASED KITCHEN

Though this collection focuses on "meaty" dishes, from nostalgic comfort classics to trendy contemporary dishes, lots of good-for-you ingredients are part of these recipes. If you're new to plant-based eating, here's a brief and handy guide to often-used foods you might want to keep in your pantry and refrigerator.

Beans and Legumes, Canned and Dried

A variety of canned beans in the pantry paves the way for lots of easy-to-prepare meals. If you have a pressure cooker, slow cooker, or Instant Pot, you might consider cooking beans from scratch. Despite all the newfangled plant proteins in this book, you'll still encounter good old-fashioned beans in these pages regularly. Here's a list of common beans and legumes you might like to keep on hand.

- Black beans
- Cannellini beans
- Chickpeas (garbanzo beans)
- Great northern beans
- Kidney beans
- Lentils
- Navy beans
- Pink beans
- Pinto beans
- Red beans

Plant-Based Meats

Now we return to the subject of this book, plant-based meats. Are they good sources of protein? Most definitely, yes! They provide an easy way to pack in a lot of protein. It would be unwieldy to list all the various brands and varieties on the market today—which seem to be growing by leaps and bounds—so here's just a small sampling of some popular products. See a longer list of major brands, along with their main protein sources, on page 250.

Viana Cowgirl Veggie Steaks (3.8-ounce serving) = 31g

Field Roast Sausages, any flavor (1 link) = 25g

No Evil Foods Comrade Cluck "No Chicken" (2.5-ounce serving) = 21g

Beyond Burger (1 patty) = 20g

Abbot's Butcher Spanish Smoked "Chorizo" (½ cup) = 16g

Upton's Naturals Bacon Seitan Strips (2-ounce serving) = 15g

Tofurky Plant-Based Deli Slices, Bologna Style (3 slices) = 14g

Grains

The grains you'll find most often in this book are rice, quinoa, barley, and oats. Whole grains add variety to meals and are sturdy, low-fat sources of fiber and protein, B vitamins, vitamin E, and an array of minerals.

Plant-Based Milks

It raises my hackles a bit (even though I have no idea what hackles are) when I hear objections to the use of the word "milk" for this category. Nut milks have been made for millennia, and it seems that it was acceptable to call them by that name up until the time when lobbyists were invented.

The first plant-based milk to hit the American market was soy milk, and that reigned supreme for a couple of decades, but now there are so many more choices. When a recipe in this book calls for plant-based milk, feel free to use your favorite kind, as long as it's plain (that is, not flavored) and unsweetened. By the way, there's nothing wrong with vanilla plant-based milk or any other flavor of plant-based milk; it just doesn't taste right in savory dishes. Save it for your coffee or cereal.

Among the varieties to choose from are almond, hemp, cashew, rice, soy, coconut (the beverage, not the canned variety), and oat milk. The latter is praised as the most sustainable and environmentally friendly of the plant-based milks.

Many plant-based milks come in aseptic containers, which means you can keep them in the pantry until they're opened, after which they need to be refrigerated.

Nuts and Seeds

In conversations about plant protein, it's sometimes easy to forget about nuts and seeds. They're a powerhouse source of healthful fats, vitamins (especially B vitamins and vitamin E), and minerals. You don't need a lot of nuts and seeds to reap their benefits; in fact, moderation is a good rule.

In this book's recipes, you'll come across almonds, cashews, peanuts, and walnuts. Seeds that are called for from time to time include sesame, sunflower, and pumpkin. You don't necessarily have to keep all these nuts and seeds on hand as pantry staples unless you plan to use them often. Otherwise, purchase them in small quantities as needed, especially during the warm months, when they can become rancid.

Pasta and Noodles

Pasta is still one of the most useful (and economical) pantry staples. This book has an entire chapter devoted to pasta, and in other chapters you'll find recipes that call for various Asian noodles. Gluten-free pastas have improved greatly over the past few years, if gluten is a concern for you.

Keep a few of your favorite short pasta shapes on hand, such as twists and shells, as well as longer noodles, such as spaghetti. You can get all kinds of Asian noodles in well-stocked supermarkets these days; these include rice noodles, soba, udon, and yakisoba. Some Asian noodles are naturally gluten-free. Consult labels, of course.

Tofu, Tempeh, and Seitan: The Original Plant-Based Protein Trio

Tofu is a superb food to add to your protein repertoire. In addition to being a good source of protein, tofu made with calcium sulfate provides up to 20% of your average daily calcium requirement. It's also low in fat and is a good source of iron and B vitamins. Here's a brief lexicon of the most common tofu varieties:

Silken Tofu

Unlike the tub variety of tofu, silken tofu, the most widely available of which is the Mori-Nu brand, comes in 12.3-ounce aseptic packages. That means

Spicy Udon Stir-Fry with Ground & Cabbage, page 110

SEITAN

A traditional Asian food used as a meat substitute, seitan appears in dishes such as Buddha's delight and Mongolian "beef" in Chinese restaurants. Dense and chewy, this product of cooked wheat gluten is almost pure protein, making it one of the most protein-dense plant foods available. An average 4-ounce serving contains 28 grams of protein. For comparison, 4 ounces of extra-firm tofu contain 8 to 10 grams of protein.

Seitan's meaty texture lends itself to numerous preparations. It's great as a substitute for beef chunks in stews, stir-fries, fajitas, and kebabs. It's great on the grill, too.

Of course, seitan isn't for anyone with gluten intolerance or sensitivity, so steer clear if that applies to you!

TEMPEH

Tempeh (pronounced *tem*-pay), made of cooked and fermented soybeans, is a traditional food of Indonesia that has long been adopted in the West as a good source of plant-based protein. It's a higher-protein cousin of tofu, with about 20 grams per 4-ounce serving.

Because of its more distinct flavor and mouth feel, tempeh may not be as endlessly versatile as tofu, but it's no slouch. It's more of an acquired taste, sometimes compared to mushrooms or chicken, but neither really describes it. If you take a liking to it, you'll find tempeh quite useful. It's sold in 8-ounce cellophane-wrapped packages, and though you're more likely to find it in natural foods stores, it has made its way into supermarkets as well—look for it in the produce section, shelved near tofu.

Page 73

it's shelf-stable, so it's good to keep a couple of cartons in the pantry. It comes in firm and extra-firm, though honestly, there's not much difference between them. Either variety makes a fantastically smooth and silky base for soups and sauces, and I call for it throughout this book.

Firm or extra-firm tofu: Most often available in 14-ounce tubs, use this kind of tofu when you want the tofu to hold its shape. It's ideal for use in stir-fries or for making cutlets or nuggets.

Baked tofu: Usually available in 5.5- to 8-ounce packages, this kind of tofu is firmer than the tub variety and comes already flavored, in contrast to the above, blander varieties. SoyBoy and WhiteWave are two brands that offer delicious baked tofu varieties including teriyaki and Caribbean flavors, and there are others as well.

Soy Sauce and Tamari

Soy sauce and tamari are useful staples; you can choose one or the other. Natural soy sauce (shoyu) is fermented and has a full-bodied flavor; it's made of soybeans, roasted wheat, and sea salt. Tamari is also naturally fermented and has a slightly stronger flavor; it also comes in a gluten-free variety. All varieties of soy sauce will keep nearly indefinitely when stored at room temperature. If sodium is a concern, choose a reduced-sodium variety (which still contains plenty of sodium).

Tomato Products

If you're not into growing your own tomatoes and/or canning them (if you are, you have my full respect), it's useful to keep a few canned tomato products on hand for use in soups, stews, and sauces. Listed below are the varieties I call for most frequently.

- Diced, in 14-ounce cans (fire-roasted or Italian-style tomatoes have extra flavor)
- Crushed or pureed, in 14-ounce and 28-ounce cans
- Tomato sauce

Other Pantry Staples

Below are a few other items you'll see used regularly in my recipes. Keep them handy or buy them as needed, depending on the types of recipes you gravitate to and the size of your pantry.

- Apple cider vinegar
- Barbecue sauce (unless you prefer to make your own)
- Coconut milk (14-ounce cans; I prefer light rather than full-fat)
- Extra-virgin olive oil
- Squeeze-bottle ginger (if you're tired of fresh ginger that's dry and stringy, this is a great alternative; look for it in the produce section of well-stocked supermarkets)
- Indian simmer sauce (see page xxii)
- Maple and/or agave syrup
- Nutritional yeast
- Peanut satay sauce (unless you prefer to make your own; see page 88)
- Salsa
- Sesame oil
- Sriracha or other hot sauce

SEASONING BLENDS

Like most people who enjoy cooking, I have a too-large collection of seasonings. In recent years, I've grown to favor seasoning blends—the kind that combine lots of herbs and spices in one bottle. They provide an efficient route to concentrated flavors. I probably have the same bottle of marjoram I bought in the 1990s, but I go through my barbecue-seasoning blends and salt-free all-purpose seasoning blends with alarming regularity. Following are my favorites.

- **Barbecue seasoning:** This spice blend is found in several varieties in the spices section of well-stocked supermarkets. McCormick Grill Mates is one of the most popular brands; other brands can be found in specialty stores or online. These seasoning blends are fantastic flavor boosters for plant proteins. Varieties include smokehouse maple, mesquite, chipotle, brown sugar bourbon—and there are lots of others. Discover your favorites and keep a couple on hand.

- **Italian seasoning:** A blend that can include marjoram, thyme, rosemary, savory, sage, oregano, and/or basil, depending on the brand, this adds fantastic flavor to soups, stews, and pasta.

- **Salt-free seasoning:** These savory blends, combining lots of herbs and spices, reduce the need for salt, both in cooking and at the table. My favorite supermarket variety is Mrs. Dash Table Blend. From the natural foods store, the aptly named Spike is a great brand, as is Frontier. This kind of seasoning blend adds a big boost of flavor to soups, stews, and many other kinds of dishes.

A FEW LINGERING QUESTIONS

What About Soy Protein Isolate and Soy Protein Concentrate?

Soy is one of the only plant foods that contains all twenty-two of the essential amino acids, making it a complete protein. Soybeans are cheap, easy to grow, and relatively sustainable, especially when compared to the land, water, and energy needed to produce animal protein. The argument that it's more "natural" to eat meat than soy becomes moot when you realize that most of the soybeans grown in the United States go toward feeding animals.

Soy protein isolate and soy protein concentrate have had a controversial history because they are highly processed foods. It's hard to deny that other forms of soy, those closer to the plant source itself—such as tofu, tempeh, edamame, and miso—are preferable. However, it has never been proved that soy protein isolate and soy protein concentrate are harmful or unhealthful (unless you have a soy allergy), especially when consumed in moderation.

If you're concerned about these kinds of processed ingredients, it's still possible to enjoy the plant-based proteins we'll be exploring in this book because many products are made without them. The majority of recipes present the option to use traditional proteins (tofu, tempeh, and seitan) in addition to or instead of meat analogs. And when you make your own plant proteins (as discussed in chapter 9), you'll know exactly what goes into them!

Is Pea Protein Better Than Soy Protein?

The use of pea protein has increased exponentially over the past few years as some of the big plant-based meat producers have come to favor it over soy. According to the Belgium-based pea protein supplier Cosucra, quoted in a report in *Nutritional Outlook* magazine, "Pea protein will remain a leading specialty vegetable protein in its own

INDIAN SIMMER SAUCE
A FLAVOR-FILLED GAME CHANGER

To create the kinds of complex flavors characteristic of authentic Southeast Asian dishes, Indian simmer sauces have been a game changer. One of the newest kinds of ready-made sauces on the market, they're available in the Asian foods section of well-stocked supermarkets and natural foods stores.

These sauces also come in a range of dairy-free varieties, including Goan coconut, Kashmir curry, jalfrezi, rogan josh, and Madras curry, with flavors ranging from mild to spicy. Some varieties do include dairy products, so be sure to read the labels if you're going full-on plant-based. Dairy-free varieties are primarily based on coconut milk and/or tomato, ginger, garlic, and lots and lots of spices. These sauces will infuse your homemade curries with the delicious flavors you've come to love at fine Indian restaurants.

Available brands will vary from one region to another, but a couple that I like are Maya Kaimal and Patak's. Trader Joe's has some good varieties, too.

right, with significant nutritional and sustainability advantages above and beyond many other plant proteins."

Pea protein is derived from yellow peas. It's easy to digest and rich in iron, and isn't a major allergen. Though pea protein is not quite as high in protein as soy, it comes close, and it is actually richer in some of the essential amino acids.

An added advantage of pea protein compared to soy and other proteins (plant or otherwise) is its environmental sustainability. It uses less water, land, and energy for an equivalent protein yield. That's something we can all celebrate.

Why Do Vegans and the Veg-Curious Want to Replicate the Foods They Gave Up?

Some readers of this book might identify themselves as omnivores exploring a plant-based diet rather than full-time vegans (though I hope that it will find some of its audience among the community). But whichever camp you belong to, you may encounter the above question, which comes up often.

The simple answer is this: a taste for meat, or meaty foods, is often acquired early in life and reflects cultural leanings. It's often quite difficult to give up these kinds of emotionally charged foods, so it's fantastic to have so many options for replacing them.

Then there's the powerful pull of nostalgia. When asked—each Thanksgiving, it seems—whether I'm on board with what's often called "tofu turkey," I always say yes. Even though my personal preference is for stuffed squash, I fully understand why people want to have a plant-based turkey substitute at the holiday table. By the way, what's often referred to as tofu turkey is more commonly known now as plant-based holiday roast. The Tofurky brand was the pioneer, which may be how the term "tofu turkey" came about in the first place.

Page 135

Many people who go vegan, or want to, do so not so much because they dislike meat but because of the myriad other good reasons for giving it up. If meals with meaty flavors and textures help more people achieve this goal, then why not?

In this introduction, I've mainly focused on what's happening in the North American market, but the skyrocketing growth of plant-based protein is a worldwide phenomenon. While traveling, I've enjoyed Sweden's Oumph and Germany's Veganz products, both of which are incredibly popular in Europe. Veganism is growing in the United Kingdom at a pace faster than that of the United States. Consult HappyCow.com before you go anywhere and you'll be presented with a plethora of options for eating out or food shopping vegan style. Pulled oats, anyone? This Norwegian product is just one of the plant proteins being developed all over the world.

I've been around long enough to remember when just being a vegetarian made me a weirdo. It's been so gratifying to witness veganism's relatively fast journey from the fringe to the forefront. Even if you're just starting to explore, more power to you, and welcome to the movement!

CHAPTER 1
SOUPS & STEWS

I LOVE SOUPS AND STEWS. In fact, I love them so much that I devoted an entire book to the subject (*Vegan Soups and Hearty Stews for All Seasons*, 2009). It started out vegetarian, and it was updated to vegan at around the same time I made the switch in my own diet. Back in the day, indignant cooks were always asking how soup could possibly be made to taste good without using a meat stock.

This no longer seems to be a question, because soup enthusiasts have come to realize that while a good stock adds depth of flavor to soups, it's the fresh and flavorful ingredients that really elevate them. And there are many soups that have been vegan from the get-go—think tomato-based soups such as minestrone and, in many cases, lentil soups.

So it's a bit of a twist that I've come around to purposely creating plant-based versions of meaty soups and stews. I say "purposely" because even when I thought I wasn't doing that, I was! For example, for as long as I can remember I've been making a vegan version of chicken noodle soup (using baked tofu) as well as what my kids used to call a "meat and potatoes" stew made with seitan. This chapter presents updated versions of recipes like these featuring a broad array of protein options as well as a slew of global classics that prove just how satisfying a plant protein–powered soup can be.

ITALIAN WEDDING SOUP

USUALLY, A WEDDING COMES *after* a relationship is underway, but with the first recipe in this collection, the nuptials will happen right out of the gate. Actually, though, the notion that this soup is traditionally served at Italian weddings is a myth. "Italian wedding soup" is a mistranslation of *minestra maritata*, or "married soup," referring to the marriage of meat (most often meatballs, but sometimes sausage) and greens in the soup.

Because at its heart this is a vegetable soup, it's easy to swap the real-meat meatballs in favor of the plant-based variety; the marriage of flavors and textures remains a beautiful love affair in a bowl.

VARIATION

Sometimes this soup cries out for pasta. If you want to stretch the number of servings, add 6 to 8 ounces of cooked pasta. Choose a small shape, like tiny shells or ditalini, cook separately, then add to the soup when adding the spinach and parsley. You'll have to adjust the amount of water as well as the seasonings, especially if you have leftovers that have been refrigerated.

1 (12- to 16-ounce) package plant-based meatballs or ½ recipe Plant-Powered Meatballs (page 227)

2 tablespoons extra-virgin olive oil

1 large or 2 medium onions, finely chopped

3 cloves garlic, minced

3 celery stalks, diced

2 medium carrots, peeled and sliced, or 1 cup chopped baby carrots

4 cups water

1 large or 2 regular-size vegetable bouillon cubes

1 (14-ounce) can diced fire-roasted tomatoes, undrained

2 teaspoons Italian seasoning

1 medium zucchini, quartered lengthwise and sliced

1 (15-ounce) can cannellini or great northern beans, drained and rinsed

2–3 big handfuls greens (whole baby spinach or arugula leaves; chopped kale, chard, or escarole)

¼ cup chopped fresh parsley

Salt and freshly ground pepper to taste

Dried hot red pepper flakes (optional)

Easy Plant Parmesan (page 243) or vegan mozzarella-style shreds for topping (optional)

1 Prepare the meatballs according to package directions (or make the DIY version), then set aside, covered, until needed.

2 Heat the oil in a soup pot. Add the onion and sauté over medium-low heat until translucent. Add the garlic, celery, and carrots and continue to sauté until all are golden and soft, 5 to 8 minutes.

3 Add the water, bouillon cubes, tomatoes, and Italian seasoning. Bring to a slow boil, then add the zucchini and beans. Turn down the heat and simmer gently for 5 to 7 minutes longer, or until the zucchini is tender but not overdone.

4 Stir in the greens and cook until just tender—a minute or so for the spinach or arugula and just a bit longer for the sturdier greens. Stir in the parsley.

5 If the soup is too crowded, add a bit more water, then season with salt and pepper. If time allows, let stand off the heat for half an hour or so to allow the flavors to develop, then heat through.

6 To serve, ladle the soup into individual serving bowls, then divide the meatballs among each bowl. Pass around dried hot red pepper flakes for those who'd like more heat as well as Easy Plant Parmesan or vegan mozzarella-style shreds for topping the soup.

SAUSAGE, POTATO & ESCAROLE SOUP

SERVES 6

A SIMPLE ITALIAN CLASSIC, this soup is incredibly warming and comforting. Escarole is a sturdy green that's too tough for salads, yet it cooks quickly and becomes almost meltingly tender in broth. Its slight bitterness is tempered by cooking as well. When prepared with cannellini beans, the soup has an almost buttery scent and flavor. Plant-based sausage and white beans join forces to make this a main-dish soup that's delicious when paired with fresh bread.

VARIATIONS

As a substitute for the escarole, use an equivalent amount of green chard, leaves chopped and stems thinly sliced.

In place of parsley, pass around your favorite vegan pesto to dollop on individual servings (or make your own Very Green Pesto, page 244).

---

2 tablespoons extra-virgin olive oil, divided

1 (14-ounce) package vegan sausage or 4 links Savory Sausage (page 230), sliced about ½ inch thick

1 large onion, quartered and thinly sliced

2 to 3 cloves garlic, minced

3 medium yellow or red-skinned potatoes, scrubbed and diced

4 cups water

1 large or 2 regular-size vegetable bouillon cubes

1 (14-ounce) can diced fire-roasted or Italian-style tomatoes, undrained

1 (15-ounce) can cannellini beans, drained and rinsed

2 teaspoons Italian seasoning

1 medium head (about 8 ounces) escarole, coarsely chopped and rinsed

½ cup chopped fresh parsley, divided

Salt and freshly ground pepper to taste

---

1 Heat 1 tablespoon oil in a medium skillet. Add the sausage and sauté over medium heat until lightly browned on most sides. Cover and set aside.

2 Heat the remaining oil in a soup pot. Add the onion and sauté over medium heat until translucent. Add the garlic and continue to sauté until both are golden, stirring frequently.

3 Add the potatoes, water, bouillon cubes, tomatoes, beans, and Italian seasoning. Bring to a slow boil, then turn the heat down and simmer gently until the potatoes are nearly done, about 15 minutes.

4 Stir in the escarole and ¼ cup parsley, then cover and simmer gently for 5 to 7 minutes, or until the escarole is tender.

5 Add more water as needed. The soup should be dense but not overly crowded. Add the remaining parsley, then season with salt and pepper. Stir in the reserved sausage.

6 If time allows, let the soup stand off the heat for an hour or so to allow the flavors to develop, then heat through.

LENTIL VEGETABLE SOUP
WITH BACON / AND A SAUSAGE VARIATION

SERVES 6

LENTILS ARE A FORCE to be reckoned with in the legume world, not only for their protein content but also for their earthy flavor. A small amount of smoky plant protein takes this robust soup from excellent to exceptional. It's one of those soups that's perfect to make on a chilly Sunday for enjoyment during the week ahead.

VARIATION

This soup also tastes good with plant-based sausage instead of bacon or tempeh. You'll need two links, finely chopped. Sauté them as you would the bacon.

2 tablespoons extra-virgin olive oil

1 large or 2 medium onions, finely chopped

2 to 3 cloves garlic, minced

3 medium carrots, peeled and thinly sliced, or 1 cup chopped baby carrots

2 large celery stalks, finely diced

7 cups water

1 large or 2 regular-size vegetable bouillon cubes

2 medium yellow potatoes or 1 large sweet potato, scrubbed and diced

1 heaping cup dried green or brown lentils, rinsed

1 (15-ounce) can diced fire-roasted tomatoes, undrained

1 tablespoon salt-free seasoning

2 teaspoons sweet or smoked paprika

2 teaspoons ground cumin

1 (5-ounce) package plant-based bacon or ½ recipe Smoky Tempeh Strips (page 224), finely chopped

Salt and freshly ground pepper to taste

¼ cup chopped fresh parsley, or more to taste

¼ cup chopped fresh dill or parsley

1 Heat the oil in a soup pot. Add the onion and sauté over medium heat for 5 minutes, or until translucent. Add the garlic, carrots, and celery and sauté for 3 to 4 minutes longer.

2 Add the water followed by the bouillon cubes, potatoes, lentils, tomatoes, seasoning blend, paprika, and cumin. Bring to a slow boil, then lower the heat, cover, and simmer until the lentils and vegetables are tender but not overdone, about 30 minutes.

3 While the soup is simmering, sauté the plant-based bacon in a medium skillet, stirring often, until lightly browned. Cover and set aside until needed.

4 When the soup is done, stir in the bacon. Adjust the consistency with more water if the soup is too dense, but let it stay nice and thick.

5 Season with salt (you may not need much) and pepper. If time allows, this soup benefits from allowing it to stand for an hour or so before serving to allow the flavors to develop. You may need to add more water as the soup stands. Heat through as needed, and stir in the fresh herbs just before serving.

CHICK'N & BLACK BEAN
TORTILLA SOUP

SERVES 6 TO 8

THIS CLASSIC SOUTHWESTERN SOUP features many of the ingredients and flavors you love in chili but in a brothy soup rather than a thick stew. Chicken is most often used in the real-meat version of this soup, but we can easily substitute chicken-style plant protein.

The fun flourish is a topping of thin strips of corn tortilla. And while these are easy to make, lo and behold, prepared corn tortilla strips are now available in small packages, the perfect quantity for distributing among several bowls of soup.

PLANT PROTEIN OPTIONS

Chicken-style plant protein, any flavor

½ recipe Chicken-Style Seitan Cutlets (page 222)

Baked tofu

2 tablespoons extra-virgin olive oil, divided

8 to 12 ounces chicken-style plant protein (see options at left), chopped fairly small

1 large or 2 medium onions, chopped

2 to 3 cloves garlic, minced

5 cups water

1 medium bell pepper, any color, diced

2 cups cooked fresh or thawed frozen corn kernels

1 (15-ounce) can diced tomatoes, preferably fire-roasted, undrained

1 (15-ounce) can tomato sauce

1 (15-ounce) can black beans, drained and rinsed

1 or 2 jalapeño peppers, seeded and chopped

2 teaspoons ground cumin

2 teaspoons chili powder

¼ to ½ cup chopped fresh cilantro, plus more for garnish

Salt and freshly ground pepper to taste

GARNISHES

6 corn tortillas, 12 mini tortillas, or 1 (3.5-ounce) package tortilla strips

1 medium ripe avocado, pitted, peeled, and sliced

1 Heat 1 tablespoon oil in a soup pot over medium heat. Add the plant protein and sauté until lightly browned on most sides, stirring often, 8 to 10 minutes. Transfer to a bowl, cover, and set aside.

2 Add the onion and garlic to the pot and sauté over medium heat until golden.

3 Add the water along with the remaining ingredients except the cilantro, salt, and pepper. Bring to a slow boil, then lower the heat, cover, and simmer gently for 15 minutes.

4 Adjust the consistency with more water if it is too thick. Stir in the cilantro and season with salt and pepper.

5 While the soup is cooking, cut the tortillas into strips about ¼ inch wide by 2 inches long. Heat a large skillet to medium-high heat, coat with a little olive oil, then add the tortilla strips. Toast, turning frequently, until dry and crisp, then transfer to a plate to cool. (Skip this step if you're using ready-made tortilla strips.)

6 Ladle the soup into serving bowls and garnish with the tortilla strips, cilantro, and a few slices of avocado.

CHICK'N NOODLE
SOUP

SERVES 6

CHICKEN NOODLE SOUP FROM a can was standard fare during my childhood. And you know how it is—even if the foods from our childhood weren't that great, the pull of the past is strong.

I've been making variations of mock chicken noodle soup for some time. But using plant protein as a chicken substitute isn't mere mockery: rather, it's the evolution of a familiar food. This simple soup lets you enjoy all the nostalgic pleasure of chicken noodle soup minus the can and the bird. It's every bit as soothing and comforting, if not even more so, because compassion is delicious!

PLANT PROTEIN OPTIONS

Chicken-style plant protein, any flavor

½ recipe Chicken-Style Seitan Cutlets (page 222)

Baked tofu

2 tablespoons extra-virgin olive oil

2 large celery stalks, finely diced

3 medium carrots, peeled and thinly sliced

2 to 3 cloves garlic, minced

1 medium onion, finely chopped

6 cups water

1 large or 2 regular-size vegetable bouillon cubes

1 tablespoon vegan poultry seasoning or salt-free seasoning

4 to 6 ounces tiny pasta, such as anellini, or short, fine noodles, such as angel hair, broken into 2-inch lengths

8 to 12 ounces chicken-style plant protein, chopped fairly small (see options at left)

Salt and freshly ground pepper to taste

2 to 3 tablespoons finely chopped fresh dill

1 Heat the oil in a soup pot. Add the celery, carrots, garlic, and onion. Sauté over medium heat for about 10 minutes, stirring often, or until the vegetables have softened and are turning golden.

2 Add the water, bouillon cubes, and seasoning and bring to a slow boil. Lower the heat, cover, and simmer gently for 10 minutes.

3 Add the noodles and chicken-style protein and return to a simmer. Cook until the noodles are al dente, 5 to 8 minutes.

4 Season with salt and pepper and stir in the dill. Serve at once.

NOTE: *As the soup stands, the noodles quickly absorb the liquid. If you plan on having leftovers of the soup, add a cup or so of additional water before storing and adjust the seasonings. This way the soup can develop more flavor as it stands.*

NEW ENGLAND
CLAMLESS CHOWDER

SERVES 6

NOW YOU CAN BE the change you want to see in the sea. The planet's oceans are being decimated by pollution and overfishing, so a number of culinary entrepreneurs have heeded the call to create plant-based seafood. This soup is the first of around a dozen in this book that use these products.

I don't believe that plant-based clams are on the market now (nor do I think anyone will be "clam-oring" for them anytime soon). Instead, this soup calls for plant-based tuna, which makes a sufficiently fishy substitute in this creamy, potato-based American classic.

1½ tablespoons extra-virgin olive oil

1 large onion, finely chopped

4 medium yellow potatoes, scrubbed and finely diced

3 medium carrots, peeled and thinly sliced

1 large or 2 regular-size celery stalks, diced

4 cups water

1 large or 2 regular-size vegetable bouillon cubes

2 teaspoons salt-free seasoning

1 (12.3-ounce) package firm silken tofu

2 cups plain unsweetened plant-based milk, divided, plus more as needed

2 cups cooked fresh or thawed frozen corn kernels

1 (4- to 6-ounce) package or can vegan tuna, flaked, or 1 (4- to 5-ounce) package plant-based crabless cakes, chopped

¼ to ½ cup chopped fresh parsley, divided

Salt and freshly ground pepper to taste

Oyster crackers for topping (optional)

1 Heat the oil in a soup pot. Add the onion and sauté over medium heat until golden.

2 Add the potatoes, carrots, celery, water, bouillon cubes, and seasoning. Bring to a slow boil, then lower the heat, cover, and simmer gently for 15 minutes, or until the vegetables are just tender and the potatoes are easily pierced with a fork.

3 Meanwhile, puree the tofu with 1 cup of the plant-based milk in a food processor or blender until creamy and smooth.

4 Add the tofu puree to the soup pot along with the corn, plant-based tuna, and half the parsley.

5 Add the remaining plant-based milk, plus more as needed if the broth is too crowded. Season with salt and pepper and continue to simmer over very low heat for 5 to 10 minutes.

6 If time allows, let the soup stand off the heat for an hour or so before serving, then heat through. Garnish servings with the remaining parsley and oyster crackers, if desired.

VIETNAMESE PHO

SERVES 6

A POPULAR CONTEMPORARY SOUP from Vietnam, pho presents a pleasing composition of rice noodles and fresh herbs in a simple broth. The customary protein in this soup is beef, which is easily omitted in favor of beef-style plant protein. Seitan works quite well in this soup, too. It's a quick soup to prepare—you'll be eating in around half an hour. A lovely change of pace from thick cold-weather soups and stews, this is light enough to be enjoyed year-round.

PLANT PROTEIN OPTIONS

Plant-based beefy strips or tips

Seitan

⅓ recipe Traditional Beef-Style Seitan (page 219)

1 (3- to 4-ounce) bundle thin rice noodles

2 tablespoons safflower or other neutral vegetable oil, divided

8 ounces beefy plant protein, cut into thin strips (see options at left)

1 medium onion, finely chopped

3 to 4 cloves garlic, minced

6 cups water

1 large or 2 regular-size vegetable bouillon cubes

2 teaspoons grated fresh or squeeze-bottle ginger, or more to taste

1 cup fresh mung bean sprouts, plus more for topping

4 scallions, thinly sliced, divided

¼ cup fresh cilantro leaves, divided

2 teaspoons freshly squeezed lime juice, or more to taste

2 tablespoons soy sauce, or to taste

Freshly ground pepper to taste

GARNISH
Lime wedges

1. Cook the noodles according to package directions until al dente, then drain and cut into shorter lengths suitable for soup. Set aside until needed.

2. Meanwhile, heat 1 tablespoon oil in a small soup pot. Add the beefy strips and sauté over medium heat until lightly browned on most sides, stirring often. Transfer to a bowl; cover and set aside.

3. Heat the remaining oil in the same pot. Add the onion and sauté over medium heat until translucent. Add the garlic and continue to sauté until both are golden.

4. Add the water, bouillon cubes, and ginger. Bring to a slow boil, then lower the heat, cover, and simmer gently for 7 to 8 minutes.

5. Stir the beefy strips into the soup along with 1 cup sprouts, half the scallions, and half the cilantro. Season with lime juice, soy sauce, and pepper. Simmer for 2 minutes longer, then remove from the heat.

6. Top each serving with a wedge or two of lime, the remaining scallions and cilantro, and a few sprouts. Serve at once.

THAI TOM KHA GAI
SOUP

SERVES 6

I FELL IN LOVE with this coconut-based vegetable soup at a Thai restaurant in my community. Because it's hard to find some of the traditional ingredients (lemongrass, galangal, Thai basil) in my local stores, I rely on plenty of ginger and lime for this homemade version, and it still hits the spot!

Thai eateries offer a choice of proteins in this soup, one of which is plain, unadorned tofu. That's my personal favorite, though this recipe gives you the option of using meatier plant proteins. Try it with a different variety each time you make it and see which you like best.

PLANT PROTEIN OPTIONS

Plant-based chick'n strips or chunks

½ recipe Chicken-Style Seitan Cutlets (page 222)

1 (14-ounce) tub firm or extra-firm tofu, well blotted and diced

1 tablespoon safflower or other neutral vegetable oil

1 medium onion, quartered and thinly sliced

2 to 3 cloves garlic, minced

2 medium carrots, peeled and sliced

1 medium bell pepper, any color, diced

6 to 8 ounces white, cremini (baby bella), or shiitake mushrooms, cleaned, stemmed, and sliced

2 cups water

2 (14-ounce) cans light coconut milk

Juice of 1 lime

2 to 3 teaspoons grated fresh or squeeze-bottle ginger

2 scallions, thinly sliced

1 teaspoon sriracha or other hot sauce, or to taste

10 to 14 ounces chicken-style plant protein (see options at left)

Salt and freshly ground pepper to taste

GARNISHES
Cilantro leaves

Lime wedges

1 Heat the oil in a small soup pot. Add the onion and sauté over medium heat until translucent. Add the garlic, carrots, bell pepper, and mushrooms and continue to sauté until all have softened, about 8 minutes. Add a little water to the pot if it becomes dry.

2 Add the water and bring to a simmer. Stir in the coconut milk, lime juice, and ginger and return to a simmer. Lower the heat, cover, and simmer gently for 10 minutes, or until the vegetables are tender but not overdone.

3 Stir in the scallions, sriracha, and plant protein. Season with salt and pepper. Continue to cook just until piping hot, then serve at once, garnished with cilantro and lime wedges.

MASSAMAN
CURRY

SERVES 4 TO 6

MASSAMAN CURRY, A THAI and Indian fusion dish, could be described as the Asian version of all-American beef-and-vegetable stew, with several ingredients that are similar. It's the base where the two stews part ways. This one is rich with coconut milk, peanut butter, and lime juice. In addition, I cross cultural boundaries and use one of my favorite shortcuts—Indian simmer sauce. These incredibly delicious sauces, available in the Asian foods aisles of most well-stocked supermarkets, are a lifesaver for those of us who are too timid (or lazy, in my case) to use the countless spices that give complex flavors to Southeast Asian–style dishes. And depending on the amount of hot sauce or paste you use, the soup can be left mild or made super spicy, as you prefer.

Traditional massaman curry is made with a variety of proteins—chicken, beef, and even duck—but here we dispense with the animals while keeping the assortment of options.

PLANT PROTEIN OPTIONS

Chicken-style or beef-style plant protein chunks

Seitan

⅓ recipe Traditional Beef-Style Seitan (page 219)

VARIATION

Replace two of the potatoes with a medium-large sweet potato, peeled and diced.

1 tablespoon extra-virgin olive oil or other vegetable oil, divided

8 to 12 ounces plant protein of your choice, cut into bite-size chunks (see options at left)

1 medium onion, finely chopped

2 to 3 cloves garlic, minced

4 medium golden or red-skinned potatoes, scrubbed and diced

1 cup water

8 ounces fresh green beans, trimmed and halved, or frozen cut green beans, thawed

1 (12-ounce) jar Indian simmer sauce (see note at right)

1 (14-ounce) can light coconut milk

¼ cup natural smooth peanut butter

Juice of 1 lime

1 to 2 teaspoons Thai red curry paste or sriracha

Salt and freshly ground pepper to taste

¼ cup fresh cilantro leaves, plus more for garnish

FOR SERVING
Cooked white rice, such as jasmine

Chopped peanuts or peanut halves

Thinly sliced scallions

NOTE: *For a spicy dish, use Madras curry; for a milder flavor, use rogan josh or jalfrezi. Make sure to choose one that's dairy-free!*

Recipe continues

1 Heat ½ tablespoon oil in a soup pot. Add the plant protein and sauté over medium-high heat until it starts to turn golden on most sides. Transfer to a plate or bowl.

2 Heat the remaining oil in the same pot and add the onion. Sauté over medium heat until translucent, then add the garlic. Continue to sauté until the onion is golden.

3 Add the potatoes and water. Bring to a slow boil, then lower the heat and simmer for 10 minutes.

4 Add the green beans and continue to simmer until they're crisp-tender and the potato is fork-tender.

5 Add the simmer sauce, coconut milk, peanut butter, and lime juice. Return to a simmer.

6 Taste and add curry paste or sriracha. Season with salt and pepper, then stir in the cilantro.

7 To serve, ladle into individual serving bowls and top with extra cilantro. Serve with hot cooked rice and sprinkle with peanuts and/or scallions, if desired.

ROGAN JOSH
CURRY

SERVES 4 TO 6

LAMB IS THE MOST commonly used red meat in Indian cuisine. The plant-based world hasn't specifically invented vegan lamb (which would be weird), so any beef-style plant protein will do as a replacement.

Rogan josh means "red lamb," and the red color in the traditional version of this dish comes from the dried red chilies of Kashmir. Their fire is tempered by cream; in this version, we'll use vegan yogurt or sour cream.

That said, this stew can be as mild or spicy as you like. Ready-made rogan josh simmer sauce is a mild, tomato-based sauce that's easy to find in the Asian foods section of well-stocked supermarkets. Green beans are my addition, but to my mind, any dish tastes better with something green in it. Serve with fresh flatbread to soak up the delicious sauce.

PLANT PROTEIN OPTIONS

Plant-based beefy chunks

Seitan

⅓ recipe Traditional Beef-Style Seitan (page 219)

1½ tablespoons safflower or other neutral vegetable oil, divided

12 to 16 ounces beef-style plant protein or seitan (see options at left), cut into bite-size chunks

1 medium onion, finely chopped

2 to 3 cloves garlic, minced

4 medium yellow potatoes, scrubbed and diced

2 cups water

8 ounces fresh or thawed frozen green beans

1 (12-ounce) jar rogan josh Indian simmer sauce

2 teaspoons grated fresh or squeeze-bottle ginger

Sriracha or other hot sauce to taste (optional)

Fresh cilantro leaves for garnish

Plain vegan yogurt or vegan sour cream for garnish

1 Heat half the oil in a small soup pot or stir-fry pan. Add the plant protein and sauté over medium-high heat, stirring often, until golden on most sides. Transfer to a bowl or plate.

2 Heat the remaining oil in the same pan. Add the onion and sauté over medium heat until translucent. Add the garlic and sauté until both are golden.

3 Add the potatoes and water. Bring to a slow boil, then lower the heat and simmer for 5 minutes. Add the green beans and continue to simmer until they and the potatoes are tender but not overdone, 8 to 10 minutes longer.

4 Add the simmer sauce and ginger. Add a bit more water if needed, though the stew should remain fairly thick. Simmer over low heat for 5 minutes longer. If you want a spicier stew, add sriracha to taste.

5 Garnish each serving with cilantro and vegan yogurt.

MOROCCAN-STYLE
CHICK'N STEW

SERVES 6 TO 8 **THIS FRAGRANT STEW IS** a wonderful way to enjoy the characteristic flavors and ingredients of Moroccan cuisine—including carrots, tomatoes, dried fruit, chickpeas, and cinnamon. Replacing the chicken customarily used in this stew is easy to do—even baked tofu does a fine job. This dish is traditionally served over couscous, but I suggest quinoa as a more flavorful and higher-protein option.

PLANT PROTEIN OPTIONS

Plant-based chick'n strips or tenders

½ recipe Chicken-Style Seitan Cutlets (page 222)

Baked tofu

2 tablespoons extra-virgin olive oil, divided

8 to 12 ounces chicken-style plant protein, cut into strips (see options at left)

1 large red onion, chopped

2 to 3 cloves garlic, minced

2 cups water

1 large or 2 medium sweet potatoes, peeled and cut into ¾-inch chunks

4 medium carrots, peeled and sliced about ¼ inch thick

1 (15-ounce) can diced fire-roasted tomatoes, undrained

1 (15-ounce) can chickpeas, drained and rinsed

2 teaspoons ground cumin

1 teaspoon ground cinnamon

½ teaspoon ground turmeric

¾ cup dried apricots, cut in half

½ cup chopped fresh parsley, divided

Salt and freshly ground pepper to taste

FOR SERVING

1 cup uncooked couscous or quinoa (optional)

Recipe continues

1 Heat 1 tablespoon oil in a soup pot. Add the plant-based chick'n and sauté over medium heat until golden brown on most sides. Transfer to a bowl or plate and set aside.

2 In the same pot, heat the remaining oil. Add the onion and sauté over medium heat until translucent. Add the garlic and continue to sauté until the onion is golden.

3 Add the water, followed by the sweet potatoes, carrots, tomatoes, chickpeas, cumin, cinnamon, and turmeric. Bring to a slow boil, then lower the heat. Cover and simmer gently for 15 minutes, or until the vegetables are tender.

4 Stir in the chick'n, apricots, and half the parsley. Season with salt and pepper and simmer over very low heat for 5 to 10 minutes longer.

5 If you want to serve this over couscous or quinoa, start cooking the grain while the stew is simmering. For couscous, combine the grains in a heatproof container with 2 cups boiling water; cover and let stand for 5 minutes, then fluff with a fork. For quinoa, combine the grains with 2 cups water in a small saucepan, bring to a slow boil, then lower the heat and simmer until the water is absorbed, about 15 minutes.

6 To serve, place a small amount of cooked grains (if desired) in the bottom of shallow bowls, then ladle some stew over it. With or without grains, sprinkle with the remaining parsley and serve at once.

BEEFY VEGETABLE STEW
WITH AN IRISH VARIATION

SERVES 6 TO 8

I'VE BEEN MAKING THIS traditional "meat and potatoes" stew for many years. The wine makes it even better, but you can leave it out if you prefer. You can also make it a plant-based rendition of Irish stew by substituting Guinness stout for the wine. Give it a try both ways and see which you prefer.

I've most often made this dish with seitan, which is still an ideal protein for it. Now, of course, there are other beefy plant-based options available.

PLANT PROTEIN OPTIONS

Plant-based beefy tips or chunks

Seitan

½ recipe Traditional Beef-Style Seitan (page 219)

VARIATION

To give this an Irish accent, replace the wine and about ½ cup of the broth with a cup of Guinness stout.

2 tablespoons extra-virgin olive oil, divided

16 ounces beef-style plant protein (see options at left), cut into bite-size pieces

1 large onion or 2 medium onions, quartered and thinly sliced

2 to 3 cloves garlic, minced

3 cups vegetable broth or 1 large or 2 regular-size vegetable bouillon cubes dissolved in 3 cups water, or more if necessary

2 teaspoons salt-free seasoning

1 teaspoon dried thyme

4 to 5 medium yellow potatoes, scrubbed (or peeled) and diced

4 medium carrots, peeled and sliced

½ cup dry red wine

3 tablespoons tomato paste

Salt and freshly ground pepper to taste

Chopped fresh parsley for garnish

1. Heat 1 tablespoon oil in a large soup pot. Add the plant protein and sauté over medium-high heat until nicely browned on most sides, stirring often. Transfer to a bowl or plate, cover, and set aside.

2. Heat the remaining oil in the same pot and add the onion. Sauté over medium heat until translucent, then add the garlic and continue to sauté until both are golden.

3. Add the broth, seasoning blend, thyme, potatoes, carrots, wine, and tomato paste. Bring to a slow boil, then lower the heat, cover, and simmer gently for 20 to 25 minutes, or until the potatoes and carrots are tender. Use the back of a wooden spoon to mash enough of the tender potatoes to thicken the stew.

4. Stir in the reserved plant protein. Add a bit more broth if needed; the consistency should be thick and moist but not soupy.

5. Season with salt and pepper (use salt sparingly, if at all), then serve in shallow bowls. Pass the parsley around the table for garnishing.

CLASSIC
BEEFY VEGETABLE CHILI

SERVES 6 TO 8

WAY BACK WHEN I first moved to New York City, there were only a handful of old-school "health food" restaurants catering to persnickety eaters like me. Already a devout vegetarian back then (veganism was a virtually unknown concept), I went into one of these restaurants one day and ordered the vegetarian chili. I called the waiter to my table not once but twice to say that I'd been given the meat chili. Finally, in exasperation, he had to bring out a bag of TVP (textured vegetable protein, also known as TSP, or textured soy protein) to prove that the chili really was meatless. It was my inauspicious introduction to scary-realistic meatless chili.

Since then, vegan chili—made with just beans and veggies and with or without some sort of textured protein—has become quite commonplace. That's why I debated whether the world needs another vegan chili recipe. But as you see, I decided in favor of including it, especially for those just stepping into the plant-based world. It's too much of a classic to leave out, especially now that there are so many ways to add protein to chili that are tastier than plain TVP.

If you want to use one of the ground recipes found in chapter 9 as your protein option, prepare it before starting the recipe.

PLANT PROTEIN OPTIONS

1 cup dry pea-protein crumbles, rehydrated

Plant-based crumbles or ground

Beef-style vegan burgers, crumbled

1 recipe Tempeh and Walnut Ground (page 214)

2 tablespoons extra-virgin olive oil, divided

8 to 10 ounces plant-based crumbles or ground (see options at left)

1 large onion, chopped

3 to 4 cloves garlic, minced

1 medium green bell pepper, diced

1 (28-ounce) can black beans, drained and rinsed

1 (28-ounce) can red beans, drained and rinsed

1 (28-ounce) can crushed tomatoes

2 cups cooked fresh or thawed frozen corn kernels

1 to 2 jalapeño peppers, seeded and minced

1 tablespoon good-quality chili powder, or to taste

1 tablespoon barbecue seasoning, any variety

1 teaspoon dried oregano

1 cup water

Salt to taste

GARNISHES

Chopped fresh cilantro

Diced ripe fresh tomatoes

Shredded vegan Cheddar- or pepper Jack–style cheese

1 Heat 1 tablespoon oil in a large soup pot. Add the plant protein of your choice and sauté over medium-high heat, stirring often, until golden brown here and there. Transfer to a bowl and set aside.

2 Heat the remaining oil in the same pot. Add the onion and garlic and sauté over medium heat until the onion is golden.

3 Add the bell pepper, beans, tomatoes, corn, jalapeños, chili powder, barbecue seasoning, oregano, and water. Simmer gently, covered, for 30 minutes, stirring occasionally. Stir in the sautéed protein, season lightly with salt (you may not need much, if any), and adjust the other seasonings.

4 If time allows, let stand for an hour or so off the heat, then heat through before serving. The chili should remain thick, but if needed, add ½ to 1 cup additional water and reheat. Ladle into serving bowls and pass the garnishes at the table.

BEEFY BARLEY & BEAN
STEW

SERVES 8 TO 10

THE CLASSIC TRIO OF barley, beans, and beef is usually presented as a soup, but to my mind, its stick-to-your ribs texture makes it more of a stew. Even after you prepare it, the barley continues to absorb the broth as it stands, so why fight it? You may need to add more water after refrigerating, but let it stay nice and thick.

The first time I made this, I reached into my pantry for a can of diced tomatoes and realized I didn't have any. With the stew already started, I used a jar of salsa instead. It adds so much flavor that I made that last-minute swap permanent. As for beans, use your favorite kind or whatever you have in the pantry—red, pink, and black beans, as well as cannellini, all work beautifully. This stew yields a heaping helping of comfort, perfect for cold winter days.

PLANT PROTEIN OPTIONS

Plant-based beefy tips or chunks

Seitan

⅓ recipe Traditional Beef-Style Seitan (page 219)

2 tablespoons extra-virgin olive oil

1 large or 2 medium onions, chopped

2 to 3 cloves garlic, minced

5 cups water, or more if necessary

1 large or 2 regular-size vegetable bouillon cubes

¾ cup uncooked pearl barley

3 to 4 medium carrots, peeled and sliced

2 medium yellow potatoes or 1 medium-large sweet potato, peeled and diced

2 large celery stalks, diced

1 tablespoon sweet paprika

1 tablespoon salt-free seasoning

1 (16-ounce) jar prepared salsa

8 to 12 ounces beef-style plant protein (see options at left), cut into bite-size chunks

1 (15-ounce) can beans of your choice, drained and rinsed

¼ cup chopped fresh parsley

2 tablespoons minced fresh dill or 1 teaspoon dried dill

Salt and freshly ground pepper to taste

1 Heat the oil in a soup pot. Add the onions and sauté over medium heat until translucent. Add the garlic and continue to sauté until both are golden.

2 Add the water, bouillon cubes, barley, carrots, potatoes, celery, paprika, seasoning blend, and salsa. Bring to a slow boil, then lower the heat. Cover and simmer gently for 40 to 45 minutes, or until the barley and vegetables are tender.

3 Meanwhile, sauté the plant protein in a lightly oiled medium skillet over medium-high heat until golden brown on most sides. Cover and set aside.

4 When the vegetables are tender, add the protein, beans, parsley, and dill to the pot. Adjust the consistency with more water if the stew has gotten too thick. Season with salt and pepper, then simmer for 5 to 10 minutes over low heat.

5 Serve at once or, if time allows, let the stew stand off the heat for an hour or so, then heat through before serving.

CHAPTER 2

SKILLETS, CASSEROLES & OTHER BAKED DISHES

THERE'S NOTHING LIKE old-fashioned casseroles and skillet dishes to conjure up images of happy housewife-moms of the 1950s—images, we now know, that were mostly fantasies. Women of that era often felt trapped and unfulfilled, so perhaps concocting these kinds of cozy meals was a small but satisfying creative antidote to their discontent.

The just-meaty-enough skillets and casseroles presented in this chapter range from the truly midcentury (Mom's "Tuna"-Noodle Casserole) to the thoroughly contemporary (Jamaican Jerk Skillet or Bowls). Filling and hefty, these kinds of dishes are still superbly comforting, and comfort is something everyone craves in our complicated world.

CLASSIC
MEAT LOAF

SERVES 8 TO 10

LET'S KICK OFF THIS chapter with a true American classic. I recommend using a plant-based beefy ground that's more moist than crumbly to achieve a cohesive texture. That will make the finished loaf easy to slice. Under the plant protein options below, you'll see that I also include a whole-foods variation made entirely of beans and walnuts.

Putting this recipe together is super easy and doesn't take much time, but a bit of patience is needed for slow baking in the oven. As for the glaze, it's optional, but I highly recommend it. It uses some of the same ingredients that go into the loaf and gives a nice finishing touch. Serve with your favorite vegetable sides—mashed potatoes and something green—for a traditional plate. It's a retro meal made contemporary and completely satisfying.

PLANT PROTEIN OPTIONS

Plant-based beefy ground (not crumbles)

1 (15-ounce) can red beans, drained and rinsed, mixed with ½ cup finely ground walnuts (if using this option, increase bread crumbs by ¼ cup)

1 tablespoon extra-virgin olive oil

1 medium onion, very finely chopped

½ medium bell pepper, any color, very finely chopped

2 to 3 cloves garlic, minced

16 ounces plant-based beefy ground (see options at left)

1 cup tomato sauce

2 tablespoons maple or agave syrup

2 tablespoons soy sauce

1 tablespoon barbecue seasoning, such as mesquite or smoky maple

2 teaspoons Italian seasoning

⅔ cup quick-cooking oats

1 cup fine bread crumbs

Freshly ground pepper to taste

FOR THE GLAZE (OPTIONAL)

¾ cup tomato sauce

1 tablespoon soy sauce

1 tablespoon maple or agave syrup

1 teaspoon barbecue seasoning

1   Preheat the oven to 350ºF.

2   Oil a 9- by 5-inch loaf pan and cover the bottom with parchment paper if desired.

3   Heat the oil in a medium skillet. Add the onion and sauté over medium heat until translucent. Add the bell pepper and garlic and continue to sauté until the onion and garlic are golden, about 8 minutes.

4   In a large mixing bowl, combine the skillet mixture with the remaining ingredients. Work together thoroughly with a large spoon or clean hands.

5   Transfer the mixture to the prepared loaf pan. Using your hands, spread the mixture to all corners of the pan and pat the top smooth. Cover with foil and bake for 1 hour.

6   To make the glaze, combine all ingredients in a small bowl and stir. Spread evenly on top of the partially cooked loaf. Bake for an additional 20 to 30 minutes, uncovered, or until the loaf looks firm and you can see browning around the edges.

7   Remove from the oven and let the loaf stand for about 15 minutes. Loosen the loaf around the edges with a knife. Invert onto a plate or cutting board, then invert again onto a serving dish. Use a sharp knife to cut into 8 to 10 slices.

BEEFY HOLIDAY PORTOBELLO POT ROAST

SERVES 6 TO 8

YOU NEED NOT WAIT for a special occasion to serve this plant-based rendition of an American classic. With its festive flair, it might just be the thing to win over skeptics who think that holidays aren't complete without a meat dish.

Portobello mushrooms amplify the meatiness of the beefy plant protein. The vegetables are roasted separately to bring out their best flavor. Brussels sprouts are usually not part of this dish, though now that I've made this a few times, I can't imagine it without them. That said, if you're not a brussels sprouts fan, substitute broccoli florets or green beans.

PLANT PROTEIN OPTIONS

Plant-based beefy tips or chunks

Seitan

⅓ recipe Traditional Beef-Style Seitan (page 219)

FOR THE BEEF AND PORTOBELLOS

1 tablespoon extra-virgin olive oil

¼ cup all-natural steak sauce or vegan Worcestershire sauce (see note on page 34)

¼ cup tomato sauce or good-quality natural ketchup

¼ cup dry red wine or vegetable broth

1 tablespoon salt-free seasoning

8 to 12 ounces beef-style plant protein (see options at left), cut into bite-size chunks

2 portobello mushrooms, stemmed, cleaned, halved, and sliced

6–8 sprigs fresh thyme, plus more for garnish

FOR THE VEGETABLES

1½ tablespoons extra-virgin olive oil

1 large or 2 medium onions, cut into bite-size chunks

2 to 3 cloves garlic, sliced

8 ounces baby carrots, cut in half lengthwise if thick

8 ounces brussels sprouts, halved

2 pounds small red-skinned or new potatoes, scrubbed

2 teaspoons salt-free seasoning

Salt and freshly ground pepper to taste

Recipe continues

1 Preheat the oven to 425°F.

2 Cover the bottom of two small roasting pans with parchment paper.

3 Heat the oil, steak sauce, tomato sauce, wine, and seasoning blend in a large skillet or stir-fry pan. Add the protein and cook over medium heat until it's touched with golden spots here and there and glazed nicely.

4 Stir in the mushrooms and 6 or so sprigs of thyme, then transfer to one of the prepared roasting pans.

5 Meanwhile, combine the ingredients for the roasted vegetables in a mixing bowl and stir together. Transfer to the other prepared roasting pan.

6 Bake the two mixtures at the same time—the protein and portobellos for 20 to 25 minutes, or until the portobellos are wilted and the protein is nicely roasted, and the vegetables for 25 to 30 minutes, or until lightly browned here and there and just tender on the inside, stirring occasionally. After 25 minutes, remove the protein and portobellos from the oven and arrange them in the center of a large shallow casserole dish (oval or round is ideal). Cover to keep warm.

7 When the vegetables are done, arrange them around the roasted protein.

8 Discard the baked thyme sprigs, garnish with fresh thyme sprigs, and serve at once.

NOTE: *Traditional Worcestershire sauce contains anchovies. Although vegan Worcestershire sauce exists, it can be a challenge to find.*

The notion of "vegan steak sauce" might seem strange, but it can easily be found in your supermarket. Make sure to choose one that contains natural plant-based ingredients, no high-fructose corn syrup, and a reasonable amount of sodium.

BEEFY STUFFED PEPPERS
WITH QUINOA & CORN

SERVES 6

STUFFED PEPPERS IN THEIR most basic form are filled with rice and ground meat. This comfort classic has evolved to the point where the stuffing options are almost unlimited—beans, grains, tofu, tempeh, vegetables, and lately, of course, the new kinds of plant proteins.

This recipe gives you a triple dose of plant protein from the quinoa, black beans, and plant-based beefy ground. You've got lots of options for the latter—you can make your own or use your favorite packaged variety—perhaps classic beef-flavored or chorizo-flavored for a bit of extra spice.

For a dish that's festive enough to serve at any special occasion, use three different shades of bell peppers—I like red, orange, and yellow.

PLANT PROTEIN OPTIONS

Plant-based beef-flavored or chorizo-flavored ground

2 cups Tempeh and Mushroom Chorizo (page 215)

2 cups Teriyaki-Flavored Ground (page 218)

6 medium bell peppers, any color or assorted colors

1½ cups cooked quinoa

8 ounces plant-based beef-flavored or chorizo-flavored ground (see options at left)

1 cup canned black beans, drained and rinsed

2 cups cooked fresh or thawed frozen corn kernels

3 scallions, thinly sliced

¼ to ½ cup chopped fresh parsley or cilantro

1 tablespoon extra-virgin olive oil (optional)

2 teaspoons ground cumin

2 teaspoons salt-free seasoning

1 teaspoon Italian seasoning

1 teaspoon smoked or sweet paprika, or to taste

Salt and freshly ground pepper to taste

1 Preheat the oven to 400°F.

2 Cut the tops off of the bell peppers. Alternatively, cut the peppers in half lengthwise, making "boats." Either way, remove the seeds and membranes.

3 If leaving the peppers whole, arrange them in a baking dish that will hold them snugly upright. You can also cut a sliver off the bottoms so they'll stand more securely. If you've cut them into halves, arrange them open side up in a casserole dish.

4 In a mixing bowl, combine the remaining ingredients and stir. Stuff the peppers generously with this mixture. Don't worry if there's some left over—you can warm it in a skillet and serve it as a tasty side dish.

5 Cover the casserole dish with its lid if it has one or foil if it doesn't. Bake for 20 minutes, then uncover and bake for 15 minutes longer, or until the peppers are tender but not collapsed. Serve at once.

SWEET POTATO
SHEPHERD'S PIE

SERVES 8 TO 10

SHEPHERD'S PIE IS ALREADY pure comfort when made with white or yellow potatoes, but it becomes even more blissful when topped with sweet potatoes. A filling of beefy ground, black beans, and corn provides a great flavor and visual contrast with the beautiful orange topping. This could be just the thing for impressing your host or guests at your next Thanksgiving or Christmas dinner!

PLANT PROTEIN OPTIONS

Plant-based beefy ground

Beef-style vegan burgers, crumbled

1 recipe Walnut, Grain, and Mushroom Crumbles (page 216)

FOR THE TOPPING

4 medium or 3 large sweet potatoes (about 3 pounds)

2 tablespoons vegan butter

½ cup plain unsweetened plant-based milk

Salt to taste

Pinch of nutmeg (optional)

FOR THE FILLING

1 tablespoon extra-virgin olive oil

1 large or 2 medium onions, finely chopped

½ medium bell pepper, any color, finely chopped

2 cloves garlic, minced

8 to 10 ounces plant-based beefy ground (see options at left)

1 (15-ounce) can black beans, drained and rinsed

1 cup cooked fresh or thawed frozen corn kernels

1½ cups prepared barbecue sauce

2 teaspoons salt-free seasoning or barbecue seasoning

¼ cup chopped fresh parsley or cilantro

Freshly ground pepper to taste

1 Prick the potatoes all over with a knife or fork. Cook on high in the microwave until soft, 5 to 7 minutes depending on the size of the potatoes. Alternatively, preheat the oven to 425°F. Wrap the potatoes in foil and bake for 45 minutes to 1 hour, or until soft. When cool enough to handle, peel and discard the skins.

2 Combine the sweet potatoes in a shallow bowl with the vegan butter (if the potatoes are no longer hot, melt the vegan butter in a saucepan or microwave it in a small bowl). Add the plant-based milk and mash until the potatoes are smooth and fluffy. Season with salt; add a pinch of nutmeg if desired, then cover and set aside until needed.

3 Preheat the oven to 375°F.

Recipe continues

4 Heat the oil in a medium skillet. Add the onion and sauté over medium heat until translucent. Add the bell pepper and garlic and continue to sauté until the onion is golden.

5 Add the beefy ground, beans, corn, barbecue sauce, seasoning, parsley, and pepper. Cook for 6 to 7 minutes over medium-high heat, or until everything is well blended and piping hot.

6 Lightly oil a 2-quart (preferably round or oval) casserole dish or two deep-dish pie plates. Pour in the ground-and-bean mixture, then spread the sweet potato mixture evenly over the top with a silicone spatula.

7 Bake for 35 to 40 minutes, or until the potatoes begin to turn golden and slightly crusty. Let stand for 5 to 10 minutes, then cut into squares or wedges to serve.

VARIATION

Arrange half the ground-and-bean mixture in a lightly oiled quiche pan or large pie plate, then distribute the remaining ingredients among individual lightly oiled ramekins. Top with the potato mixture and bake as directed above.

TEX-MEX
CHICK'N & RICE
CASSEROLE

SERVES 4 TO 6 **THIS CONTEMPORARY TAKE ON** a classic casserole is a crowd-pleasing dish filled with familiar flavors and a favorite among eaters of all ages and inclinations. It tastes wonderful made with brown or white basmati rice, which fills your kitchen with a delicious aroma as the casserole bakes. It's also a great way to use up leftover cooked rice.

Black bean and corn salsa is delicious in this dish; for extra spiciness, use a chipotle-flavored salsa. Any flavor of salsa other than a fruity variety works well.

PLANT PROTEIN OPTIONS

Plant-based chick'n chunks or strips

½ recipe Chicken-Style Seitan Cutlets (page 222)

1 recipe Crazy Easy Chickpea Chick'n (page 225)

Baked tofu

1 tablespoon extra-virgin olive oil

1 medium yellow or red onion, chopped

2 cloves garlic, minced

½ bell pepper, any color, diced

8 to 11 ounces chicken-style plant protein (see options at left), cut into bite-size pieces

4 to 4½ cups cooked long-grain brown or white rice

1 cup cooked fresh or thawed frozen corn kernels

1 (8-ounce) package vegan cheese shreds, preferably pepper Jack–style

½ cup vegan sour cream, plus more for serving

2 teaspoons ground cumin

1 cup prepared salsa, plus more for serving

¼ cup chopped fresh cilantro

Salt and freshly ground pepper to taste

1 Preheat the oven to 375ºF.

2 Heat the oil in a medium skillet. Add the onion and sauté over medium-low heat until translucent. Add the garlic, bell pepper, and plant protein and continue to sauté until the onion and plant protein are golden and starting to brown lightly here and there.

3 In a large mixing bowl, combine the skillet mixture with the remaining ingredients. Stir together, then transfer to an oiled shallow 1½-quart baking dish. Bake for 30 to 35 minutes, or until the top is golden and the casserole is starting to turn crusty along the edges.

4 Remove from the oven and let the casserole stand for a few minutes. Cut into squares to serve; pass extra salsa and sour cream at the table for garnishing.

CHICK'N POT PIE
CASSEROLE

SERVES 8

ALL THE COMFORTING FLAVORS of pot pie come together in this casserole, which yields more generous servings than the original. Instead of a pastry crust, a cobblerlike crust covers the vegetables. To serve, you can flip the portions onto the plate so that the crust sits on the bottom—but that's entirely up to you.

Use three or four different kinds of vegetables in this dish. It takes on a different personality depending on what you have on hand. This recipe is an ideal way to use up small amounts of vegetables lurking in your refrigerator or freezer.

PLANT PROTEIN OPTIONS

Plant-based chick'n chunks or strips

½ recipe Chicken-Style Seitan Cutlets (page 222)

1 recipe Crazy Easy Chickpea Chick'n (page 225)

Baked tofu

FOR THE FILLING
2 medium-large yellow or red-skinned potatoes

1 tablespoon extra-virgin olive oil

1 medium onion, chopped

8 ounces plant-based chick'n (see options at left), finely chopped

4 cups steamed vegetables (see options on page 41)

1 cup vegetable broth or plain unsweetened plant-based milk

2 teaspoons poultry seasoning

¼ cup chopped fresh parsley

Salt and freshly ground pepper to taste

FOR THE TOPPING
1¼ cups whole wheat pastry flour

½ teaspoon baking powder

1 teaspoon salt

1 cup plain unsweetened plant-based milk

1 tablespoon extra-virgin olive oil

1 Prick the potatoes all over with a knife or fork. Cook on high in the microwave until soft, 5 to 7 minutes depending on the size of the potatoes. Alternatively, preheat the oven to 425ºF. Wrap the potatoes in foil and bake for 45 minutes to 1 hour, or until soft. When cool enough to handle, peel and discard the skins. The potatoes can be prepared to this point up to a few hours or a day ahead of time.

2 Dice one of the potatoes; coarsely mash the other.

3 Preheat the oven to 375ºF.

4 Heat the oil in a stir-fry pan or large skillet. Add the onion and sauté over medium heat until translucent. Add the chick'n and continue to sauté until both are golden and touched with brown spots here and there, 8 to 10 minutes.

5 Add the diced and mashed potatoes, steamed vegetables, broth, and poultry seasoning. Stir together and cook briefly, just until everything is well blended and warm.

Broccoli, cut into small florets

Brussels sprouts, trimmed and quartered

Butternut squash, finely diced

Carrots or baby carrots, thinly sliced

Cauliflower, cut into small florets

Corn kernels

Green beans, cut into 1-inch pieces

Green peas, no more than ½ cup

Mushrooms, cleaned, stemmed, and sliced

Zucchini or yellow summer squash, diced

6 Stir in the parsley and season with salt and pepper. Pour the mixture into a lightly oiled shallow 1½- to 2-quart baking dish.

7 To make the topping, combine the flour, baking powder, and salt in a small mixing bowl and stir together. Make a well in the center and add the plant-based milk and oil. Stir together just until completely blended.

8 Spread the batter evenly over the vegetable mixture with the help of a spatula or large spoon.

9 Bake for 35 minutes, or until the batter is golden and firm. Remove from the oven and let stand for 5 to 10 minutes. To serve, cut into squares or wedges, or just scoop out with a large spoon.

MOM'S "TUNA"-NOODLE
CASSEROLE

SERVES 6

THIS VEGAN VERSION OF old-fashioned tuna-noodle casserole takes the dish straight from the 1950s into the present day and beyond. Traditionally, this recipe uses canned soups or flour-thickened sauces. Here we'll dispense with both those options in favor of a creamy base made with white beans and plant-based milk.

The few steps involved in preparing this recipe can be accomplished in the time it takes to heat up the water for the pasta and cook it. Pack leftover portions of this casserole in brown-bag lunches—it's just as tasty at room temperature as it is served warm.

VARIATION

While this recipe is meant to highlight plant-based tuna, you can easily substitute an equivalent amount of finely diced or crumbled baked tofu.

---

8 to 10 ounces short pasta, such as shells or twists

1 (15-ounce) can cannellini or great northern beans, drained and rinsed

1 cup plain unsweetened plant-based milk

2 teaspoons salt-free seasoning

2 tablespoons olive oil or vegan butter

1 medium onion, finely chopped

3 medium celery stalks, diced

2 cups thawed frozen green peas

1½ to 2 cups vegan cheese shreds, preferably Cheddar-style

5 to 6 ounces plant-based tuna, flaked

Salt and freshly ground pepper to taste

Fine bread crumbs and paprika for garnish

---

1 Preheat the oven to 375°F.

2 Cook the pasta according to package directions until al dente, then drain.

3 Meanwhile, combine the beans, plant-based milk, and seasoning blend in a food processor or blender. Process until very smooth.

4 Heat the oil in a large skillet or stir-fry pan. Add the onion and celery and sauté over medium heat until golden and just beginning to brown lightly.

5 Pour the pureed beans into the pan along with the cooked pasta, peas, vegan cheese, and plant-based tuna. Stir together, then season with salt and pepper and stir again. If your pan threatens to spill over, combine the ingredients in a mixing bowl.

6 Transfer the mixture to an oiled 1½-quart round or rectangular casserole dish. Sprinkle with bread crumbs and paprika. Bake for 25 to 30 minutes, or until the top is golden brown. Allow to cool for 5 minutes, then dig in.

BACON BAKED BEANS

IF YOU LIKE BAKED beans, you can always open a can—some brands are naturally vegan and quite good. But they just don't compare to this homemade casserole.

While navy beans are the most traditional ingredient in baked beans, I prefer cannellini or great northern beans—larger varieties of white beans—because they offer more bean and less skin. Here they're paired with pinto or red beans for a contrast in color and texture.

If you're looking for a big, inexpensive dish to feed a crowd, feel free to double this recipe and bake in a shallow 2-quart casserole. When finished, it might not seem like a large quantity, but each serving is quite filling.

2 tablespoons extra-virgin olive oil, divided

8 strips plant-based bacon, cut into small pieces (about half of a 5- to 6-ounce package), or ½ recipe Smoky Tempeh Strips (page 224)

1 medium onion, finely chopped

2 cloves garlic, minced

1 (15-ounce) can cannellini or great northern beans, drained and rinsed

1 (15-ounce) can pinto or red beans, drained and rinsed

1½ cups Quick No-Cook Barbecue Sauce (page 240) or bottled barbecue sauce, or more to taste

Chopped fresh cilantro for garnish (optional)

1 Preheat the oven to 350°F.

2 Heat 1 tablespoon oil in a large skillet or stir-fry pan. Add the bacon and sauté over medium-high heat until lightly browned here and there, stirring often. Transfer to a plate.

3 Heat the remaining oil in the same skillet. Add the onion and sauté over medium-low heat until translucent. Add the garlic and continue to sauté until the onion is lightly browned. Stir in the beans and most of the cooked bacon; reserve a little for the topping.

4 Stir the barbecue sauce into the bean mixture. If you want a saucier dish, add a little more. It might look like too much, but it will bake into the dish.

5 Transfer the mixture to a lightly oiled 1-quart baking dish (or you can bake in individual ramekins or heatproof bowls). Bake, covered, for 30 minutes, then uncover and bake for an additional 15 minutes. Garnish with the reserved bacon and the cilantro, if desired, and serve hot.

JAMBALAYA

SERVES 6 TO 8

SPICY BITES OF VEGAN sausage jazz up this plant-based rendition of a Creole-Cajun classic. Serve with a simple coleslaw and a green vegetable (leafy greens, green beans, or brussels sprouts) for a hearty, satisfying dinner. If you want to go full-on Cajun, add plant-based shrimp or even plant-based chicken for a traditional festive meal.

VARIATIONS

Add a package of plant-based shrimp, 8 ounces of plant-based chicken, or 8 ounces of baked tofu to the mix. Cook any of these optional ingredients in the skillet along with the sausage.

Add 8 to 10 ounces of fresh or thawed frozen okra, trimmed and sliced, to the skillet with the garlic, celery, and bell pepper.

1½ cups uncooked long-grain brown rice

3½ cups water, plus more if desired

1 (14-ounce) package vegan sausage or 4 links Savory Sausage (page 230)

2 tablespoons extra-virgin olive oil

1 large onion, chopped

3 to 4 cloves garlic, minced

4 celery stalks, diced

1 medium green or red bell pepper, diced

1 (14-ounce) can tomato sauce

1 (14-ounce) can diced tomatoes, preferably fire-roasted

2 teaspoons Cajun seasoning blend or smoked paprika, or more to taste

2 teaspoons Italian seasoning

Cayenne pepper or dried hot red pepper flakes to taste

Salt and freshly ground pepper to taste

Chopped scallion and/or chopped fresh parsley for garnish

1. Combine the rice and water in a medium saucepan and bring to a rapid simmer. Reduce the heat to low and simmer gently until the water is absorbed, 30 to 35 minutes. If you prefer a more tender grain, add ½ cup additional water and cook until absorbed.

2. Cut the sausage links into ½-inch-thick slices. (You can slice them a little thinner if you like.) Heat just enough of the oil to coat the bottom of a wide skillet or stir-fry pan. Cook the sausage pieces over medium-high heat, gently turning them until most sides are golden brown. Transfer to a bowl and set aside.

3. Heat the remaining oil in the same skillet. Add the onion and sauté over medium heat until translucent. Add the garlic, celery, and bell pepper and continue to sauté until all are lightly browned.

4. Stir in the cooked rice, sautéed sausage, tomato sauce, diced tomatoes, and seasonings. Bring to a simmer, then cover and cook over low heat for 15 minutes, stirring occasionally.

5. Season to taste with cayenne, salt, and pepper. You can let this stand off the heat for a few minutes to allow the flavors to develop or serve at once. Either way, pass chopped scallion and/or parsley at the table for garnishing.

SMOKY LENTILS &
SAUSAGE / WITH YELLOW RICE

SERVES 4 TO 6

LENTILS AND SAUSAGE FORM a compatible duo in dishes that sometimes incorporate vegetables, especially greens. Because this is not the prettiest dish in and of itself, it's often accompanied by yellow rice. The preparation seems to combine several cuisines—it's a little bit Italian, a tad Spanish, and maybe even a touch Caribbean. Whatever its origins, this dish is hearty, unpretentious, and totally satisfying.

Use any variety of lentils other than tiny red lentils, which cook to mush and are best reserved for soups. Ordinary brown or green lentils do quite nicely, but you can also go with French lentils or black beluga lentils. To save time, you can even use canned lentils. Barbecue seasoning blends add a deliciously smoky flavor and aroma, but if you prefer smoked paprika, go ahead and use that instead.

NOTE: *Barbecue seasoning is available in the spice section of most supermarkets. Varieties include smokehouse maple, mesquite, chipotle, and lots of others. Discover your favorites and keep a couple on hand.*

1½ cups uncooked white basmati or jasmine rice or ¾ cup uncooked white rice and ¾ cup uncooked quinoa

3½ cups water, plus more if desired

½ teaspoon ground turmeric

1 tablespoon extra-virgin olive oil

1 (14-ounce) package vegan sausage or 4 links Savory Sausage (page 230), sliced ½ inch thick

3 cloves garlic, minced

½ medium red or orange bell pepper, finely diced

3 to 3½ cups cooked lentils or 2 (15-ounce) cans lentils, drained and rinsed

1 (14-ounce) can diced fire-roasted tomatoes

1 tablespoon barbecue seasoning or smoked paprika

2 to 3 big handfuls baby spinach

¼ cup chopped fresh parsley or cilantro

Salt and dried hot red pepper flakes to taste

1 Combine the rice (or rice and quinoa) and water in a saucepan over high heat. Bring to a slow boil, then sprinkle in the turmeric and stir to distribute. Lower the heat and simmer gently until the water is absorbed, about 15 minutes. If you prefer a more tender grain, add ½ cup additional water and cook until absorbed. Remove from the heat.

2 Meanwhile, heat the oil in a large steep-sided skillet or stir-fry pan. Add the sausage and sauté over medium heat for 5 minutes, stirring often.

3 Add the garlic and bell pepper and continue to sauté for 2 to 3 minutes longer. Add the lentils, tomatoes, and barbecue seasoning. Cook over medium-low heat for 10 minutes.

4 Stir in the spinach and parsley and cook just until wilted and bright green, a minute or so longer. Season with salt and dried hot red pepper flakes. Serve at once over the hot cooked rice.

ROASTED SASUAGE
WITH POLENTA & FENNEL

SERVES 4 TO 6

WHAT I LIKE MOST about roasted dishes is that they need little embellishment. A few vegetables, a little olive oil, and subtle seasonings are all it takes to give a dish that sought-after wow factor.

This medley of vegan sausage, precooked polenta, and fennel is a case in point. Fennel is an underappreciated vegetable that lends a delightful anise flavor to dishes. It harmonizes beautifully with the sausage, and polenta—the kind that comes in tubes—adds a major comfort factor. This can also serve as a fantastic vegan stuffing for holiday meals.

---

1 (18-ounce) tube precooked polenta

1 medium bulb fennel

1 (14-ounce) package vegan sausage or 4 links Savory Sausage (page 230), sliced ½ inch thick

6 ounces cremini (baby bella) mushrooms, stemmed, cleaned, and sliced

Extra-virgin olive oil

1 teaspoon salt-free seasoning

Salt and freshly ground pepper to taste

Sliced fresh sage leaves or whole rosemary leaves (optional)

1 Preheat the oven to 400°F.

2 Line the bottom of a large roasting pan with parchment paper.

3 Cut the polenta into ½-inch-thick slices. Then cut each round into four wedge-shaped pieces.

4 Slice the stem end off of the fennel and discard, then cut the bulb into bite-size strips. Slice the celerylike stalks into ½-inch pieces. Remove the feathery fronds and set aside.

5 Combine the polenta, fennel, sausage, and mushrooms in a large mixing bowl. Drizzle in a little oil, just enough to coat everything lightly, then sprinkle with the seasoning blend.

6 Transfer the mixture to the prepared roasting pan and roast for 25 to 30 minutes, or until everything is touched with golden brown in spots.

7 Season with salt and pepper and stir in the reserved fennel fronds. Add sage or rosemary if desired. Serve straight from the roasting pan.

SMASHED
SWEET POTATOES / WITH BEER BRATS

SERVES 4 TO 6

TRUTH BE TOLD, I'M not a fan of beer. But as I was searching for dishes to make with plant-based sausage, I kept bumping into beer brats. It seemed like some sort of sign!

Beer brats are usually served on a hero roll with sauerkraut, and I do love sauerkraut, so I decided to give them a try. The result of cooking vegan sausage in beer with a hint of sweetness and mustard was far more pleasing than I expected, but the beige-on-beige aesthetic called out for improvement. Serving the brats on sweet potatoes proved just right, providing a tasty synergy between the mellow sweet potato, savory sausage, and tart sauerkraut.

4 large sweet potatoes, well scrubbed

1 tablespoon extra-virgin olive oil

1 (14-ounce) package vegan sausage or 4 links Savory Sausage (page 230), sliced ½ inch thick

1 cup beer

1 tablespoon maple or agave syrup

2 teaspoons prepared yellow mustard

1 teaspoon Italian seasoning

Sauerkraut to taste

GARNISHES (OPTIONAL)

Thinly sliced red onion

Thinly sliced scallion

Seeded and thinly sliced jalapeño pepper

1 Prick the potatoes all over with a knife or fork. Cook on high in the microwave until soft, 5 to 7 minutes depending on the size of the potatoes. Alternatively, preheat the oven to 425°F. Wrap the potatoes in foil and bake for 45 minutes, or until soft.

2 Once the sweet potatoes are nearly done, heat the oil in a wide skillet. Add the sliced sausage and sauté over medium-high heat until lightly browned on most sides, stirring often.

3 Add the beer, syrup, mustard, and Italian seasoning and stir. It will seem like there's an excessive amount of beer, but it cooks off quickly. Bring the mixture to a simmer, then turn the heat down a bit and cook until the beer reduces, 5 to 8 minutes.

4 Once the sweet potatoes are done, cut in half lengthwise and arrange one or two halves on each serving plate. Smash the flesh lightly with a fork.

5 Distribute the sausage mixture among the potato halves and top with sauerkraut. Sprinkle with any of the garnishes, if desired, and serve.

QUICK CHILI-TOPPED SWEET POTATOES

SERVES 4 TO 6

LOADING SWEET POTATOES WITH a streamlined version of chili that includes beefy crumbles is a quick route to a satisfying emergency dinner. If you don't have the time or patience to bake whole sweet potatoes in a conventional oven (their flavor and texture do benefit from slow cooking), microwaving them is fine. Each large sweet potato (two halves) yields a hefty portion, but if you're serving this with other dishes, half a sweet potato topped with chili is quite filling.

4 large sweet potatoes, well scrubbed

FOR THE CHILI

Extra-virgin olive oil for the pan

8 to 10 ounces plant-based beefy crumbles or ground or 1 (8-ounce) package beef-style vegan burgers, crumbled

1 (15-ounce) can black or red beans, drained and rinsed

1 cup cooked fresh or thawed frozen corn kernels

1 (12-ounce) jar prepared salsa

1 (14-ounce) can diced fire-roasted tomatoes

1 tablespoon chili powder

1 tablespoon barbecue seasoning

FOR THE TOPPING

Vegan cheese shreds, preferably Cheddar- or pepper Jack–style

Thinly sliced scallions or chopped fresh cilantro

1. Prick the potatoes all over with a knife or fork. Cook on high in the microwave until soft, 5 to 7 minutes depending on the size of the potatoes. Alternatively, preheat the oven to 425°F. Wrap the potatoes in foil and bake for 45 minutes to 1 hour, or until soft.

2. When the potatoes are cool enough to handle, cut them in half lengthwise and mash the centers lightly. Alternatively, cut them down the center but don't go all the way, leaving the skin on the bottom intact so that the potatoes function as a pocket.

3. In the meantime, heat just enough oil to coat a large skillet or stir-fry pan. Add the beefy crumbles and sauté for 5 minutes over medium-high heat, stirring often.

4. Add the remaining chili ingredients and stir. Cook for 8 to 10 minutes over medium-low heat, stirring occasionally.

5. Top each sweet potato half generously with chili, followed by a sprinkling of cheese and some scallion and/or cilantro. If you want the cheese to melt completely, microwave individual portions for up to a minute.

CREAMED GREENS, CORN & BACON SMASHED POTATOES

SERVES 4

SMASHED POTATOES WITH LIGHTLY creamed (or, more accurately, mayo'd) greens and corn would be fantastic if that's where it ended, but the bacon topping takes this preparation to the next level of flavor. You'll find power greens (usually a blend of spinach, chard, and kale) shelved near baby spinach and other packaged greens in the supermarket. If you can't find them, use baby spinach. The dish will taste just as good.

4 large yellow potatoes, well scrubbed

2 teaspoons extra-virgin olive oil or other vegetable oil

8 slices packaged plant-based bacon or Smoky Tempeh Strips (page 224), cut into small bits

½ cup cooked fresh or thawed frozen corn kernels

1 (5- to 6-ounce) package power greens or baby spinach

2 scallions, sliced

¼ cup chopped fresh parsley or cilantro

⅓ cup vegan mayonnaise

Salt and freshly ground pepper to taste

1 Prick the potatoes all over with a knife or fork. Cook on high in the microwave until soft, 5 to 7 minutes depending on the size of the potatoes. Alternatively, preheat the oven to 425ºF. Wrap the potatoes in foil and bake for 45 minutes to 1 hour, or until soft.

2 When the potatoes are nearly ready, heat the oil in a large skillet or stir-fry pan. Cook the bacon over medium-high heat until lightly browned and crisp on most sides. Transfer to a plate and set aside.

3 In the same skillet, warm the corn kernels over medium heat, adding just enough water to keep the pan moist. Add the greens and cook until wilted, about 2 minutes. Drain the mixture in a colander, gently pressing out as much liquid as you can.

4 Return the mixture to the pan and set over low heat. Stir in the scallions and parsley. Stir in the mayo and season with salt and pepper.

5 Cut the cooked potatoes in half lengthwise and smash the flesh lightly with a fork. Divide the greens mixture between them, then top with the bacon. Serve at once.

JAMAICAN JERK SKILLET OR BOWLS

SERVES 4

THE KEY TO ANY Caribbean-inspired jerk dish is a good sauce, though this puts me in a quandary. I like good-quality prepared sauces, as you may be coming to learn, but I haven't found a bottled jerk sauce I completely love. They're usually way too salty. On the other hand, to make an authentic Jamaican jerk sauce requires Scotch bonnet peppers and a few other ingredients that aren't readily available. My compromise is the simple Jerk Sauce on page 237.

That said, feel free to use bottled jerk sauce, which you'll find shelved with other sauces and marinades in well-stocked supermarkets. Compare brands if you do, because you'll want one with natural ingredients and the lowest possible sodium content.

This skillet dish is light and lovely, like an ocean breeze, even if it's not totally authentic. It's a feast for the eyes and a treat for the palate, with its sweet and savory notes. It can be made with either chick'n or beef-style protein. Serve it straight from the skillet or construct pretty bowls as shown on page 58.

PLANT PROTEIN OPTIONS

Chick'n or beef-style plant protein, cut into chunks, tips, or strips

½ recipe Chicken-Style Seitan Cutlets (page 222)

Seitan

½ recipe Traditional Beef-Style Seitan (page 219)

FOR THE COCONUT RICE

1½ cups uncooked basmati rice

2 cups water, plus more if desired

1 (14-ounce) can light coconut milk

2 tablespoons extra-virgin olive oil, divided

1 large red or yellow onion, quartered and thinly sliced

1 medium red bell pepper, cut into long, narrow strips

1 medium green bell pepper, cut into long, narrow strips

12 to 16 ounces chick'n or beef-style plant protein (see options at left), cut into bite-size chunks or strips

1 recipe Jerk Sauce (page 237) or ¾ cup good-quality bottled jerk sauce

FOR SERVING

1 to 1½ cups diced fresh ripe or thawed frozen mango

1 medium ripe avocado, pitted, peeled, and diced or sliced

Chopped fresh parsley, cilantro, or basil for garnish

Recipe continues

1 Combine the rice, water, and coconut milk in a medium saucepan and bring to a slow boil. Lower the heat, cover, and simmer until the liquid is absorbed, 15 to 20 minutes. If you prefer a more tender grain, add ½ cup additional water and cook until absorbed.

2 Meanwhile, heat 1 tablespoon oil in a wide skillet or stir-fry pan. Add the onion and sauté over medium-low heat until translucent. Add the peppers and continue to cook until the onions and peppers are lightly browned. Transfer to a bowl or plate and set aside.

3 In the same skillet, heat the remaining oil. Add the plant protein and sauté over medium-high heat, stirring frequently, until golden brown on most sides.

4 Pour in the sauce, reduce the heat to medium, and cook for a minute or so longer, until the sauce has thickened and the protein is nicely glazed. Stir in the sautéed onions and peppers.

5 **To serve from the skillet:** Have everyone take some rice to use as a bed for the jerk protein. The avocado and mango are served on the side, and the herbs are sprinkled on top.

6 **To serve in bowls:** Distribute the cooked rice among 4 shallow bowls. Arrange the jerk mixture on one side of each bowl and some of the avocado and mango next to it. Sprinkle some fresh herbs over the top and serve at once.

CHAPTER 3

PROTEIN-POWERED PASTAS

MOST OF THE RECIPES in this chapter, with the exception of the last two, are Italian-inspired. If you enjoy noodle dishes, you'll find those with an Asian spin in chapter 4. Italian cuisine is filled with many vegan or almost-vegan dishes, but we'll be skipping over those here in favor of transforming meaty classics into plant-based iterations. That would seem pretty counterintuitive in a general vegan cookbook, but in this one, the goal is to show how even the meatiest fare can easily be made meatless.

If you're a fan of hearty Italian-style pasta dishes, I highly recommend preparing the Easy Plant Parmesan recipe on page 243. It gives these kinds of pasta dishes a nice finishing touch, and since it's basically made with almond flour and nutritional yeast, it adds even more protein to your meal.

BEEFY
MUSHROOM
STROGANOFF

SERVES 6 **THIS DELECTABLE AND EASY** vegan stroganoff is just as luscious as the original—and better for you, too. Perhaps it's better to describe it as a mash-up of pasta Alfredo and stroganoff. The former is a heart-stopper, featuring pasta bathed in a cream and butter sauce. Most of the original recipes I explored clock in at a whopping 40 grams of fat (or more) per serving. This recipe replaces all that butter and cream with a silken tofu–based sauce that's every bit as delicious.

Old-school stroganoff doesn't fare much better than Alfredo sauce when it comes to fat and calories. Traditional recipes call for egg noodles to be doused in sour cream and butter, then topped with mushrooms (which we'll keep) and beef. The plant-based protein-and-mushroom combo we use here is the very definition of umami!

PLANT PROTEIN OPTIONS

Plant-based beefy strips or tips

Seitan

½ recipe Traditional Beef-Style Seitan (page 219)

16 ounces pasta (see note on page 64)

FOR THE CREAMY SAUCE

1 tablespoon vegan butter or extra-virgin olive oil

2 to 3 cloves garlic, minced

1 (12.3-ounce) package firm silken tofu

½ cup plain unsweetened plant-based milk, plus more if desired

Salt and freshly ground pepper to taste

FOR THE STROGANOFF TOPPING

1 tablespoon extra-virgin olive oil

1 medium onion, quartered and thinly sliced

2 large portobello mushrooms, stemmed, cleaned, halved, and thinly sliced

8 to 10 ounces beef-style plant protein (see options at left), cut into bite-size pieces

⅓ cup sun-dried tomatoes, cut into strips

Salt and freshly ground pepper to taste

Finely chopped fresh parsley for garnish

Recipe continues

1 Cook the pasta according to package directions until al dente, then drain. While it's cooking, proceed with the next steps.

2 **For the sauce:** Melt the vegan butter in a medium skillet. Add the garlic and sauté over low heat for 2 to 3 minutes, until golden. Remove from the heat.

3 Combine the sautéed garlic with the tofu and plant-based milk in a food processor or small blender. Process until completely smooth and creamy. Season with salt and pepper and set aside.

4 **For the stroganoff topping:** Heat the oil in the same skillet over medium heat. Add the onion and sauté until golden.

5 Add the mushrooms and plant protein to the skillet. Turn the heat up to medium-high and continue to sauté, stirring often, until the mushrooms are wilted and the plant protein begins to brown lightly, about 5 minutes. Stir in the sun-dried tomatoes and remove from the heat.

6 Combine the pasta and the tofu mixture in a large serving bowl and mix thoroughly. Season with pepper and adjust salt if necessary. If the sauce is too thick, add a splash of plant-based milk.

7 To serve, distribute the mushroom and plant protein topping over individual servings of pasta. Top each serving with a sprinkling of parsley.

NOTE: *This recipe works well with fettuccine or any ribbon-type pasta, including pappardelle, whether made from traditional durum wheat, whole wheat, or spelt.*

CLASSIC RAGÙ

SERVES 6 OR MORE

RAGÙ IS A CLASSIC Italian beefy sauce that seems like a cousin to Bolognese. In the original recipe, beef is shredded (rather than ground) after it has cooked for a very long time—something that's unnecessary with plant protein. Even with the quicker cooking time, the resulting red sauce is deeply flavored and delicious. Ragù is traditionally served with ribbon pasta, but any favorite shape will work.

PLANT PROTEIN OPTIONS

12 to 16 ounces packaged steak-style or roast beef-style plant protein

Beefy tips

Seitan

½ recipe Traditional Beef-Style Seitan (page 219)

NOTE: *You can shred the protein by hand, or if it's nice and firm, you can run it through the grating blade of a food processor.*

3 tablespoons extra-virgin olive oil, divided

12 to 16 ounces beef-style plant protein (see options at left), torn into short, thin shreds (see note)

1 medium onion, finely chopped

3 to 4 cloves garlic, minced

1 cup peeled and finely chopped carrot

1 cup finely diced celery

1 (6-ounce) can tomato paste

1 (28-ounce) can crushed tomatoes, preferably Italian-style

1 cup water, plus more if desired

½ cup dry red wine or additional water

1 tablespoon Italian seasoning

Salt and freshly ground pepper to taste

Dried hot red pepper flakes to taste (optional)

16 ounces uncooked pasta, any variety

1 Heat about half of the oil in a small soup pot. Add the plant protein and sauté over medium heat, stirring often, until lightly browned. Transfer to a plate or bowl and set aside.

2 Heat the remaining oil in the same pot. Add the onion and sauté over medium heat until translucent.

3 Add the garlic, carrot, and celery and continue to sauté until all are golden and tender.

4 Add the tomato paste, crushed tomatoes, water, wine, and Italian seasoning. Bring to a simmer, then lower the heat, cover, and cook for 15 minutes.

5 Stir in the plant protein and cook for 15 to 20 minutes longer. If the sauce is too thick, adjust the consistency with an additional ½ cup of water. Season with salt, pepper, and dried hot red pepper flakes, if desired.

6 About halfway into the cooking time for the ragù, cook the pasta according to package directions until al dente, then drain.

7 Serve a generous dollop of ragù over individual servings of pasta.

PASTA
BOLOGNESE

SERVES 6

IN CLASSIC PASTA BOLOGNESE, the tomato-based sauce is generally made with ground meat, but it's so easy to prepare a vegan version. Another characteristic ingredient of Bolognese sauce is heavy cream, which is replaced here with any kind of plant-based milk or creamer. Simple and hearty, this is a great weeknight meal served with a colorful salad.

PLANT PROTEIN OPTIONS

Plant-based beefy ground or crumbles

1 recipe Walnut, Grain, and Mushroom Crumbles (page 216)

1 tablespoon extra-virgin olive oil

1 medium onion, chopped

2 to 3 cloves garlic, minced

1 medium green bell pepper, finely diced

1 large celery stalk, finely diced

10 to 12 ounces plant-based ground (see options at left)

⅓ cup dry red wine

1 (15-ounce) can diced tomatoes, undrained

1 (15-ounce) can tomato sauce

2 teaspoons Italian seasoning

1 cup water

¼ cup plain unsweetened plant-based milk or creamer

12 to 16 ounces short, chunky pasta

Salt and freshly ground pepper to taste

Thinly sliced fresh basil leaves or chopped fresh parsley for topping (optional)

Easy Plant Parmesan (page 243) or finely grated vegan Parmesan-style cheese for topping (optional)

1 Heat the oil in a large saucepan. Add the onion and sauté over medium heat until translucent.

2 Add the garlic, bell pepper, celery, and ground and continue to sauté until the mixture is touched with golden brown here and there, stirring often, about 10 minutes.

3 Add the wine, tomatoes, tomato sauce, seasoning, and water. Bring to a simmer, then cover and simmer gently for 15 minutes, stirring occasionally, until the ground is tender and infused with the tomato flavors. Turn off the heat and stir in the plant-based milk or creamer.

4 About halfway into the cooking time for the sauce, cook the pasta in plenty of rapidly simmering water until al dente, then drain.

5 When both the pasta and sauce are done, combine them in a large serving bowl and toss together.

6 Season with salt and pepper. Serve at once, passing the basil and/or Easy Plant Parmesan at the table, if desired.

BAKED
SPAGHETTI PIE

SERVES 6 TO 8

SPAGHETTI PIE IS ONE of those classic dishes that might seem a bit silly on paper, and once you've made it, you realize that it really *is* silly—but even so, it's really good. And it's one of those dishes that kids are likely to love and request. You'll be happy, too, knowing that there's a good quantity of greens in it. If you have a springform pan, you can play up the pie aspect of this dish, but any round casserole dish will do.

PLANT PROTEIN OPTIONS

Plant-based beefy ground or crumbles

4 beef-style vegan burgers, crumbled

1 recipe Walnut, Grain, and Mushroom Crumbles (page 216)

8 ounces spaghetti

1 tablespoon olive oil

1 medium onion, finely chopped

3 to 4 cloves garlic, minced

1 cup cleaned, stemmed, and chopped mushrooms

8 to 10 ounces plant-based ground or crumbles (see options at left)

1 (28-ounce) jar marinara sauce

1 (5-ounce) package baby spinach, baby kale, or power greens (see page 56)

1½ cups vegan mozzarella-style shreds, divided

Freshly ground pepper to taste

Chopped fresh parsley for garnish (optional)

1 Preheat the oven to 375°F.

2 Break the spaghetti in half and cook according to package directions until al dente, then drain.

3 Meanwhile, heat the oil in a large skillet or stir-fry pan. Add the onion and sauté over medium heat until translucent. Add the garlic and continue to sauté until the onion is golden.

4 Add the mushrooms and plant-based ground and continue to sauté over medium-high heat, stirring often, until the mushrooms are wilted and the ground is touched with golden spots here and there, 8 to 10 minutes.

5 Stir in the marinara sauce and cook until starting to simmer. Add the spinach (in batches if necessary), cover, and cook just until it wilts, then remove from the heat.

6 Add the cooked spaghetti to the pan (or combine it with the sauce in a mixing bowl if your pan isn't large enough) along with 1 cup of the vegan cheese and stir. Grind in some pepper.

7 Transfer the mixture to an oiled 1½-quart casserole dish (round or oval works well, but use what you've got) and distribute the mixture evenly with your hands. Pat the top to make it smooth. If you've got a springform pan, that will make the pie nice and firm and tall. Top with the remaining cheese.

8 Bake for 30 to 40 minutes, or until the cheese is nicely melted and the sides of the pie are starting to turn golden brown and crusty.

9 Remove from the oven, top with a sprinkling of parsley, if desired, then let stand for 5 minutes or so. If using a springform pan, remove the outer ring. Cut into wedges or squares, or simply scoop from the pan, to serve.

Baked Spaghetti Pie, page 68

PASTA
PUTTANESCA
WITH MEATBALLS

SERVES 6 TO 8

PUTTANESCA, AN OLD NEAPOLITAN pasta dish named for ladies of the night, is characterized by its briny sauce, courtesy of olives and anchovies. We, of course, dispense with the latter. If you love olives, you'll adore this pasta dish. It's not always served with meatballs, though that's far from unheard of. It's a great way to transform a dish that's light on protein into one that's more substantial.

10 to 12 ounces pasta, any shape

1 tablespoon olive oil

3 to 4 cloves garlic, minced

1 medium green bell pepper, cut into short, narrow strips

1 pound ripe fresh tomatoes, diced

1 (28-ounce) jar marinara sauce

1 cup pitted and halved black and/or green brine-cured olives

¼ cup sliced sun-dried tomatoes (optional)

Dried hot red pepper flakes to taste

1 (12- to 16-ounce) package plant-based meatballs or 1 recipe Plant-Powered Meatballs (page 227)

¼ cup chopped fresh parsley for garnish

Sliced fresh basil leaves for garnish

1 Cook the pasta according to package directions until al dente, then drain.

2 Heat the oil in a large saucepan. Add the garlic and bell pepper and sauté over medium-low heat for 2 to 3 minutes, or until the garlic is golden.

3 Add the tomatoes, marinara sauce, olives, and sun-dried tomatoes, if desired. Increase the heat to medium-high and bring to a simmer, then lower the heat and simmer gently, uncovered, for 3 to 5 minutes.

4 Combine the cooked pasta with the olive sauce in a serving bowl. Season with red pepper flakes. Cover and set aside.

5 Heat the meatballs according to package directions. You can toss them into the pasta or arrange some atop each serving, followed by a sprinkling each of parsley and basil.

ITALIAN-STYLE SAUSAGE & PEPPERS

SERVES 6

THIS HOME-STYLE ITALIAN CLASSIC is easy to update with plant-based sausage. It makes a hearty one-dish meal when served with pasta, grains, or even soft polenta. I especially like it with farro, an oft-neglected whole grain most used, appropriately, in Italian cuisine.

On the off chance that you have any leftovers, you can transform them into delicious hero sandwiches—sounds like a great lunch to me!

2 tablespoons extra-virgin olive oil, divided

1 (14-ounce) package vegan sausage or 4 links Savory Sausage (page 230), cut into ½-inch slices

1 large onion, quartered and thinly sliced

2 to 3 cloves garlic, minced

3 large red, green, and/or orange bell peppers

¼ cup dry red or white wine (optional)

1 (28-ounce) can crushed tomatoes

2 teaspoons Italian seasoning, or more to taste

¼ cup chopped fresh parsley or basil

Dried hot red pepper flakes to taste

Salt and freshly ground pepper to taste

Hot cooked pasta, grains, polenta, or hero rolls for serving

1 Heat just enough of the oil to lightly coat the bottom of a large skillet. Add the vegan sausage and cook over medium-high heat, stirring frequently, until all sides are golden brown, about 8 minutes. Transfer to a plate and set aside.

2 Heat the remaining oil in the same pan. Add the onion and sauté over medium-low heat until translucent. Add the garlic and peppers and sauté until all are soft and golden, about 8 minutes.

3 Stir in the wine, if desired, crushed tomatoes, Italian seasoning, herbs, and red pepper flakes. Bring to a simmer, then cover and cook over low heat for 10 minutes.

4 Stir the reserved vegan sausage into the mixture. Season with salt and pepper. Serve at once, spooning some of the mixture over pasta, grains, or polenta. Or arrange as much as you can comfortably fit on the bottom halves of hero rolls, then cover with the top halves.

CHICK'N TETRAZZINI
PASTA

SERVES 4

THE TRADITIONAL TETRAZZINI RECIPE combines chicken with a long pasta and a heavy cream–based sauce, which is then baked as a casserole. I've eliminated the baking step because I found that it doesn't improve the result—in fact, it detracts from it by drying it out. Cooked my way, the dish can be enjoyed as soon as it's ready. I've added a touch of "Florentine" here as well with baby spinach, which isn't usually part of the dish.

The creaminess is courtesy of silken tofu rather than heavy cream. Your heart will thank you for it; your palate will be happy, too.

PLANT PROTEIN OPTIONS

Plant-based chick'n, cut in chunks or chopped

½ recipe Chicken-Style Seitan Cutlets (page 222)

Baked tofu

1 tablespoon vegan butter

1 cup fine bread crumbs (see note)

8 to 10 ounces long pasta, such as linguine, broken in half

1 cup thawed frozen green peas, at room temperature

1 tablespoon extra-virgin olive oil

1 medium onion, quartered and thinly sliced

8 to 11 ounces plant-based chicken (see options at left), cut into bite-size chunks

3 to 4 cloves garlic, minced

6 to 8 ounces white or cremini (baby bella) mushrooms, cleaned, stemmed, and sliced

¼ cup dry white wine (optional)

¼ cup chopped fresh parsley, or more if desired

1 (12.3-ounce) package firm or extra-firm silken tofu

½ cup vegetable broth or 1 regular-size vegetable bouillon cube dissolved in ½ cup water

Salt and freshly ground pepper to taste

2 to 3 big handfuls baby spinach or baby arugula

1. Heat the vegan butter in a large skillet or stir-fry pan over medium heat. Add the bread crumbs and sauté, stirring frequently, until toasted and golden, about 8 minutes. Transfer to a plate or bowl and set aside.

2. In a large pot, cook the pasta according to package directions. Once it's al dente, plunge the peas in, then drain both at once.

3. Meanwhile, heat the oil in the pan used for the bread crumbs. Add the onion and sauté over medium heat until translucent.

4. Add the plant-based chicken, garlic, and mushrooms and continue to sauté until all are golden and starting to turn lightly brown, 8 to 10 minutes. Pour the wine, if desired, into the pan to deglaze. Stir in the parsley, remove from the heat, and cover.

5 Combine the silken tofu and broth in a food processor and process until smoothly pureed.

6 Add the puree to the pan along with the cooked pasta and peas. Return to medium heat. Stir together, then season with salt and pepper. Continue to cook just until the mixture is heated through. Add the spinach, cover, and cook until wilted, then stir.

7 Serve immediately, passing the bread crumbs at the table for topping.

NOTE: *If you don't have bread crumbs on hand, simply put two slices of whole-grain bread, torn into a few pieces, in a food processor and pulse until reduced to crumbs.*

PASTA WITH CHICK'N & EGGPLANT PARMESAN

SERVES 6

BOTH CHICKEN PARMESAN AND eggplant Parmesan are classic recipes in their original form, so why not combine the two for a vegan version? Getting your protein and vegetable goodness in a single dish is efficient as well as delicious.

Chickpea liquid, also known as aquafaba, is a perfect plant-based substitute for egg when it comes to coating foods that will then be breaded—in this case, both the chick'n and the eggplant. Make a simple salad to go with this dish using dark leafy greens, carrots, tomatoes, and peppers. Dress in a vinaigrette or any other favorite dressing.

PLANT PROTEIN OPTIONS

Plant-based chick'n strips or cutlets

½ recipe Chicken-Style Seitan Cutlets (page 222)

Baked tofu

---

1 medium eggplant

8 to 11 ounces plant-based chicken (see options at left)

1 (15-ounce) can chickpeas

¼ cup fine cornmeal

2 teaspoons Italian seasoning

10 to 12 ounces large chunky pasta, such as penne or ziti

1 (28-ounce) jar vegetable marinara sauce

½ cup chopped black olives

¼ cup chopped fresh parsley, divided

Dried hot red pepper flakes to taste

Freshly ground pepper to taste

1½ cups vegan mozzarella-style shreds

Packaged vegan Parmesan or Easy Plant Parmesan (page 243) for topping (optional)

1 Preheat the oven to 400°F.

2 Line a baking sheet or roasting pan with parchment paper.

3 Stem the eggplant and cut in half. Cut each half into ½-inch-thick rounds, then cut the rounds into half-moons. Finally, cut in the opposite direction to make narrow strips.

4 If using chick'n cutlets, cut into strips to more or less match the eggplant. If using precut chick'n strips, no need to cut further.

5 Combine the eggplant and chick'n in a mixing bowl.

6 Drain the chickpeas, reserving the liquid (aquafaba). Drizzle in 2 to 3 tablespoons of the liquid to moisten the eggplant and chick'n. Discard the remaining liquid, rinse the chickpeas, and set aside.

7 Combine the cornmeal and Italian seasoning in a gallon-size plastic bag. Add the eggplant and chick'n mixture and shake until evenly coated.

8 Transfer to the prepared baking sheet or roasting pan and bake for 20 to 25 minutes, stirring once or twice, or until the eggplant is tender on the inside and both it and the chick'n are starting to crisp on the outside.

9 Meanwhile, cook the pasta according to package directions until al dente, then drain and return to the same pot.

10 Add the drained chickpeas, marinara sauce, olives, half the parsley, red pepper flakes, and pepper to the pot with the pasta. Stir, then transfer to a lightly oiled shallow 1½-quart baking dish.

11 Arrange the breaded eggplant and chick'n over the surface of the pasta, followed by the cheese. Return to the oven for 10 minutes, or until the cheese is nicely melted.

12 Scatter the rest of the parsley over the top and serve at once. Pass the vegan Parmesan at the table, if desired.

PASTA
CARBONARA
WITH BROCCOLI

SERVES 4 **TRADITIONALLY MADE WITH PANCETTA** or salami, carbonara is a pasta dish that's easy to convert to vegan with the simple substitution of plant-based pepperoni for the pork-based kind. The dish also tastes good with vegan bacon, which is a bit easier to find than vegan pepperoni. Simple, quick, and straightforward, this is a sturdy everyday pasta dish that leaves you enough time and energy to make a colorful side salad.

NOTE: *Carbonara is traditionally made with spaghetti, but you can use fettuccine, linguine, or whatever shape you happen to have in your pantry.*

10 to 12 ounces long pasta (see note)

2 tablespoons extra-virgin olive oil, divided

5 to 6 ounces plant-based pepperoni or bacon, cut into small bits

3 to 4 cloves garlic, minced

4 to 5 cups finely chopped broccoli florets

¼ cup dry white wine, vegetable broth, or water

¼ cup chopped fresh parsley

2 to 4 tablespoons plain unsweetened plant-based creamer

Salt and freshly ground pepper to taste

Packaged vegan Parmesan or Easy Plant Parmesan (page 243) for topping (optional)

1 Cook the pasta according to package directions until al dente, then drain.

2 Meanwhile, heat 1 tablespoon oil in a wide skillet. Sauté the pepperoni pieces over medium heat until crisp and golden brown on both sides, then transfer to a small bowl.

3 In the same skillet, heat the remaining oil over low heat. Add the garlic and sauté until golden.

4 Add the broccoli and wine to the skillet. Cover and steam until the broccoli is bright green and crisp-tender, 3 to 4 minutes. Remove from the heat.

5 In a serving bowl, combine the cooked pasta, bacon, broccoli-garlic mixture (with any remaining liquid), and parsley. Toss well. Add enough creamer to give the dish a bit more moisture. Season with salt and pepper, then serve. Pass the vegan Parmesan at the table, if desired.

SMOKY BROCCOLI & BACON MAC & CHEESE

SERVES 6 TO 8

MACARONI AND CHEESE IS now a proud member of the vegan repertoire, and there are so many ways to make it. I've served it to many people who claim that they couldn't possibly go vegan because they can't give up cheese. This is a dish that proves you don't have to.

Though there's plenty of broccoli in this dish, I've snuck in extra vegetable goodness with cauliflower. It blends right in with the creamy, cheesy sauce. Plant-based bacon adds bursts of flavor, not to mention extra protein. When you need a big dish to serve at home or share at a potluck dinner, this makes a heaping helping.

16 ounces short, chunky pasta

2 medium broccoli crowns, cut into bite-size florets

Olive oil

5 to 6 ounces plant-based bacon or Smoky Tempeh Strips (page 224), cut into small bits

1 (12.3-ounce) package firm or extra-firm silken tofu

2 tablespoons vegan butter

2 heaping cups well-cooked fresh or thawed frozen cauliflower florets

1 cup plain unsweetened plant-based milk

1 (8-ounce) package vegan Cheddar-style cheese shreds

1 tablespoon barbecue seasoning

Salt to taste

1 Cook the pasta in a large pot according to package directions. Just as the pasta turns al dente, stir in the broccoli and cook for a minute or so, until it turns bright green. Drain, then return the pasta and broccoli to the cooking pot.

2 Meanwhile, heat just enough oil to coat a medium skillet. Add the bacon and cook for a few minutes over medium-high heat, stirring often, until touched with golden brown spots and turning crisp, 6 to 8 minutes.

3 Combine the silken tofu, vegan butter, cauliflower, plant-based milk, and cheese shreds in a blender. Blend until creamy and smooth.

4 Pour the sauce into the pot with the broccoli and pasta and stir. Mix in the bacon and barbecue seasoning. Cook over medium-low heat for a few minutes, until everything is piping hot and the cheese has melted.

5 Season with salt and let stand for 5 to 10 minutes to allow the pasta to absorb a bit of the sauce, then serve.

CHILI MAC

CHILI MAC IS ONE of those odd amalgams that just somehow works. This dish was once more commonly known as Cincinnati chili mac, though the Ohio city of its origin is now usually dropped from the title. Originally, the recipe consisted of a basic chili embellished with sweet spices and served over spaghetti. Contemporary versions, like this one, use short pasta shapes so that everything can be stirred up together. The result is a mash-up of chili plus mac and cheese that's uniquely American.

PLANT PROTEIN OPTIONS

Plant-based beefy ground or crumbles

½ recipe Walnut, Grain, and Mushroom Crumbles (page 216)

1 tablespoon extra-virgin olive oil

1 large onion, finely chopped

1 medium bell pepper, any color, diced

8 to 10 ounces plant-based ground (see options at left)

1 (28-ounce) can crushed tomatoes

1 (15-ounce) can kidney or pinto beans, drained and rinsed

1 jalapeño pepper, minced (optional)

1 tablespoon chili powder, or to taste

1 teaspoon ground cumin

1 teaspoon dried oregano or Italian seasoning

½ teaspoon ground cinnamon

8 to 10 ounces elbow-shaped pasta or rotini

1 to 2 cups Cheddar- or pepper Jack–style vegan cheese shreds

GARNISHES (OPTIONAL)
Sliced jalapeño peppers

Chopped fresh cilantro or parsley

1 Heat the oil in a large soup pot or stir-fry pan. Add the onion and sauté over medium heat until translucent. Add the bell pepper and sauté briefly, just until softened.

2 Add the ground and continue to sauté, stirring often, until everything is golden and beginning to brown lightly, 8 to 10 minutes.

3 Stir in the tomatoes, beans, jalapeño (if desired), chili powder, cumin, oregano, and cinnamon and bring to a simmer. Lower the heat, cover, and simmer gently for 15 minutes.

4 Meanwhile, cook the pasta according to package directions until al dente, then drain. Add the cooked pasta and cheese shreds to the pot and stir. Cook until the cheese is well melted.

5 Serve straight from the pan, passing the garnishes at the table, or transfer to a large serving bowl and top with the garnishes.

CHAPTER 4

FROM THE ASIAN TAKE-OUT MENU

IF I'M GOING TO take a break from cooking, I'm most likely to crave Asian food. So I'm pretty familiar with Asian take-out menus (I've practically got a special drawer for them!), even though I tend to order the same favorites over and over—specifically, the ones from the (usually) very short vegetables section. My eyes glaze over the rest.

Exploring meaty Asian specialties was quite an education for me, even as I realize that what's on Asian menus in the United States might bear little resemblance to the authentic dishes from their countries of origin. I mean, Mongolian beef? Buddha bowls? And though I can't compare the recipes in this chapter to their traditional counterparts, I can assure you that they're delicious in their own right. Most are as packed with veggies as they are with protein, and they land on your table in no time—sometimes in less time than it takes to order takeout.

PEANUT SATAY
SKEWERS

DON'T BE DAUNTED BY the number of ingredients and steps in this recipe—it truly is easy to make. You can even skip the skewers and it will still be impressive.

I confess that when I'm pressed for time I've substituted bottled peanut satay sauce for the ingredients below. Since you need to open a can of coconut milk for the marinade anyway, you can stir a little into the bottled sauce to improve the flavor and color and mitigate the sodium content.

My favorite way to make this is with super-firm tofu, which comes in a sealed package and isn't as watery as tub tofu But it works beautifully with many other plant protein varieties, including chick'n, tempeh, and seitan. You can try a different protein each time or combine two kinds. No matter what you use, it makes a luscious appetizer on its own or a wonderful main course when served with rice or noodles.

PLANT PROTEIN OPTIONS

Super-firm tofu (drained; no need to blot)

Extra-firm tofu (well blotted or pressed)

Plant-based chick'n (firm, thick strips work best)

Tempeh

Seitan

1 recipe Chicken-Style Seitan Cutlets (page 222)

14 to 16 ounces plant-based protein (see options at left), cut into chunky strips or large dice

Extra-virgin olive oil for the pan

FOR THE MARINADE

½ cup light coconut milk

2 cloves garlic, minced

Juice of 1 lime

2 tablespoons soy sauce (optional; see note at left)

2 tablespoons natural granulated sugar or agave syrup

Freshly ground pepper to taste

NOTE: *Skip the soy sauce in the marinade if you're using a packaged plant-based chicken product or seitan: both have enough sodium.*

FOR THE PEANUT SATAY SAUCE

⅓ cup natural smooth peanut butter

½ cup light coconut milk

Juice of 1 lime

2 tablespoons soy sauce

2 teaspoons grated fresh or squeeze-bottle ginger

½ teaspoon sriracha or other hot sauce, or to taste

2 teaspoons natural granulated sugar or agave syrup

Crushed peanuts for topping (optional)

GARNISHES

1 or 2 thinly sliced scallions

Coarsely chopped fresh cilantro

Recipe continues

1 Select a plant protein from the list on page 88 and cut it into chunky strips or large dice. Arrange it in a single layer in a shallow container or two.

2 Combine the marinade ingredients in a small bowl and stir. Pour over the plant protein and allow to marinate for at least an hour. Alternatively, cover and refrigerate overnight; the longer it stands, the more marinade the protein will absorb.

3 To make the sauce, combine the peanut butter, coconut milk, lime juice, soy sauce, ginger, sriracha, and agave syrup in a small bowl and whisk. If your peanut butter is thick and a bit too dry to whisk, you may need to combine the ingredients in a food processor and process until smooth. Pour into a single serving bowl or individual serving bowls and garnish with crushed peanuts, if desired.

4 Drain the protein and discard the marinade. Pour a drizzle of oil into a nonstick skillet or grill pan (if you want those cool grill marks)—just enough to cover the surface—and heat over medium heat. Arrange the protein in a single layer in the skillet and sauté until it begins to turn golden and crisp, 6 to 8 minutes. Turn the protein over and cook on the other side until golden, 4 to 6 minutes.

5 Thread 2 to 4 pieces of protein on skewers, if using.

6 Arrange the skewers on a serving platter and scatter the scallions and cilantro over the top. Plate with a side of the satay sauce or pass the sauce at the table. Serve warm or at room temperature.

PAD SEE EW

SERVES 4

IF YOU'VE EVER ORDERED pad see ew at a Thai eatery, you know that it always comes with a choice of meats, so here I offer various choices of plant proteins— it's always good to have options! Try using a different kind each time you make it.

Rice noodles quickly absorb this sauce and can become a bit dry if the dish stands for a while. To perk up leftovers, simply stir in a little water to moisten, then adjust seasonings to taste.

Oyster sauce is used in the traditional recipe, but of course we need to skip that here. Black bean sauce and hoisin sauce are both fine substitutes, and both give the rice noodles the brown gloss that makes the dish so appealing. I hope you enjoy this easy homemade version of pad see ew as much as we do in our house, where it's earned a spot in the semiregular rotation.

PLANT PROTEIN OPTIONS

Tofu nuggets (such as Hodo)

Plant-based chick'n chunks or strips

Plant-based fish fillets

Plant-based shrimp

Seitan

Baked tofu, diced

FOR THE SAUCE

¼ cup black bean sauce or hoisin sauce

2 tablespoons soy sauce

2 tablespoons natural granulated sugar

FOR THE NOODLES

8 ounces extra-wide rice noodles or 1 (11-ounce) package fresh precooked rice noodles (see notes on page 92)

1 tablespoon safflower or other neutral vegetable oil

8 to 11 ounces plant-based protein (see options at left), cut into bite-size chunks or strips

2 to 3 cloves garlic, minced

6 to 8 ounces Chinese broccoli, broccolini, broccoli rabe, or 1 large broccoli crown, cut into bite-size pieces

½ cup grated carrot

3 scallions, cut into 1-inch lengths

Sriracha or other hot sauce to taste, plus more for the table

Soy sauce to taste

GARNISHES

Crushed peanuts

Lime wedges

Fresh cilantro leaves or thinly sliced fresh basil

Recipe continues

1 Combine the sauce ingredients in a small bowl and whisk. Set aside.

2 Cook the noodles according to package directions. Drain and set aside.

3 Heat the oil in a large stir-fry pan. Add the protein of your choice and cook over medium-high heat until golden on most sides. When nearly done, toss in the garlic and continue to stir-fry for another minute or so.

4 Add the broccoli and grated carrot and continue to stir-fry until both are just crisp-tender, about 3 minutes.

5 Stir in the noodles, sauce, and scallions and cook just until everything is well combined and hot. Add hot sauce and additional soy sauce.

6 Top individual servings with any or all of the suggested garnishes and pass extra hot sauce at the table.

NOTES: *If extra-wide rice noodles are unavailable, use the regular kind of wide rice noodles (though not rice vermicelli). These noodles are super long, so once they're cooked, you may want to cut them here and there to shorten them a bit.*

The instructions on packages of precooked rice noodles often say to add them directly to the stir-fry. However, I find them a bit too al dente right out of the package; I recommend microwaving them for 2 minutes with a bit of water in a covered dish or combining them with hot water in a bowl and letting them stand for a few minutes.

SWEET & SOUR STIR-FRIED VEGETABLES

SERVES 6

A BIG, BEAUTIFUL SWEET and sour stir-fry is one of my favorite Asian-inspired dishes to make at home. The synergy between the colorful vegetables and the sweet pineapple is delightful. As in the recipe for Pad See Ew (page 91), the protein options are eminently flexible, and you can try a different one each time you make this. The vegetables can be varied, too, according to what's in season or what's in the fridge.

PLANT PROTEIN OPTIONS

Plant-based beefy chunks or strips

Plant-based meatballs

½ recipe Teriyaki Meatballs (page 218)

Plant-based chick'n chunks or strips

Seitan

½ recipe Traditional Beef-Style Seitan (page 219)

Tempeh

Extra-firm tofu

1 (20-ounce) can pineapple chunks in unsweetened juice

FOR THE SWEET AND SOUR SAUCE

2½ tablespoons cornstarch or arrowroot

½ cup water

¼ cup rice vinegar

2 tablespoons soy sauce

1 tablespoon natural granulated sugar

1 to 2 teaspoons grated fresh or squeeze-bottle ginger

FOR THE VEGETABLES

2 tablespoons safflower or other high-heat oil, divided

12 to 16 ounces plant protein (see options at left), cut into bite-size pieces

2 to 3 cloves garlic, minced

2 cups fresh or thawed frozen cauliflower florets

8 to 10 asparagus spears, trimmed and cut into 2-inch lengths

1 medium bell pepper, any color, cut into narrow 2-inch strips

2 medium ripe fresh tomatoes, diced

Hot cooked rice, quinoa, or noodles for serving

Sriracha or other Asian hot sauce for serving

Recipe continues

1 Drain the pineapple and reserve ½ cup of the juice.

2 In a small bowl, combine the cornstarch with just enough of the water to dissolve it. Add the remaining water, reserved pineapple juice, and the rest of the sauce ingredients and whisk. Set aside.

3 Heat 1 tablespoon oil in a stir-fry pan or wide skillet over medium-high heat. Add the plant protein and stir-fry until golden brown on most sides, stirring frequently. Transfer to a bowl or plate.

4 Heat the remaining oil in the same pan. Add the garlic and sauté over low heat until golden.

5 Add the cauliflower and stir-fry for 2 to 3 minutes. Add the asparagus and bell pepper and continue to stir-fry until the vegetables are just barely crisp-tender, 2 to 3 minutes longer.

6 Add the tomatoes, pineapple chunks, and plant protein and continue to stir-fry until everything is well heated through.

7 Whisk the sauce a bit, then pour it into the pan. Cook until it thickens. Taste to adjust the flavor balance to your liking with more sugar, vinegar, and soy sauce.

8 Serve at once over hot cooked grains or noodles. Pass the hot sauce at the table.

VARIATIONS

This stir-fry is as flexible on the vegetables as it is on the proteins. Use green beans or snow peas instead of asparagus; broccoli instead of cauliflower. You can introduce carrots or squashes into this stir-fry. It's a fantastic way to use up whatever you've got in your fridge!

SESAME CHICK'N
WITH STIR-FRIED VEGETABLES

SERVES 4

HERE'S ANOTHER TAKE-OUT FAVORITE gone plant-based. Like the recipes for chicken-style dishes, this one has several protein options to choose from, including tofu. This one, too, is completely flexible when it comes to the vegetables—as long as you use a variety of them. As with all stir-fries, have the vegetables prepped and ready to go. Once you stir up the sauce and stir-fry the protein, it all goes fast from there.

PLANT PROTEIN OPTIONS

Plant-based chick'n strips or chunks

½ recipe Chicken-Style Seitan Cutlets (page 222)

Baked tofu

FOR THE SAUCE

2 tablespoons cornstarch or arrowroot

⅓ cup water, divided

½ cup bottled teriyaki or black bean sauce or homemade Teriyaki Sauce (page 241)

2 tablespoons soy sauce

2 tablespoons natural granulated sugar

2 teaspoons grated fresh or squeeze-bottle ginger

1 teaspoon sriracha, or more to taste

FOR THE PROTEIN

1 tablespoon safflower or other neutral vegetable oil

10 to 12 ounces chicken-style plant protein (see options at left), cut into bite-size chunks

2 tablespoons sesame seeds

FOR THE VEGETABLES

1 tablespoon safflower or other neutral vegetable oil

2 to 3 cloves garlic, minced

5 to 6 cups mixed vegetables (choose any 3 or 4: trimmed snow peas, baby corn, thinly sliced carrots, small broccoli florets, bell pepper strips, diced zucchini, sliced bok choy or celery, stemmed and sliced mushrooms)

2 scallions, thinly sliced

Hot cooked rice or noodles for serving

1 In a small bowl, combine the cornstarch with about half the water, or just enough to smoothly dissolve it. Add the remaining water and the rest of the sauce ingredients, stir, and set aside.

2 To cook the protein, heat the oil in a stir-fry pan. Add the plant protein and stir-fry over high heat until golden brown on most sides, about 8 minutes.

3 Pour in about ¼ cup of the sauce and continue to stir-fry until it coats the protein nicely. Sprinkle in the sesame seeds, covering the protein as evenly as possible. Transfer to a plate or bowl and cover.

4 Wipe the pan out to remove any remaining sesame seeds.

5 To cook the vegetables, heat the oil and add the garlic. Sauté over medium-low heat for a minute, then add the vegetables. Increase the heat to high and stir-fry until everything is crisp-tender, about 5 minutes.

6 Stir in the remaining sauce and the scallions. Serve at once over rice or noodles, arranging some of the sesame-covered protein next to the vegetables.

CHICK'N & VEGETABLE CHOW MEIN

SERVES 4 TO 6

CHOW MEIN IS A decidedly Americanized version of Asian stir-fry dishes, but no matter, since it's such a nice mix of veggies and protein. In this recipe, you've got plenty of options when it comes to replacing chicken, though it's also great with ordinary tofu. Make sure to have all your vegetables cut and ready, because once the onion-and-protein mixture is done, it all goes very fast from there.

PLANT PROTEIN OPTIONS

Plant-based chick'n

½ recipe Chicken-Style Seitan Cutlets (page 222)

Baked tofu

NOTE: *Yakisoba are not the same as the crispy-cracker type of chow mein noodles sold in cans. You'll find yakisoba in the Asian foods section of well-stocked supermarkets. It's a superfine wavy wheat noodle with a nice mouth feel. If you can't find them, or if you prefer, you can substitute an equivalent amount of other long, thin noodles, including ramen and thin spaghetti.*

FOR THE SAUCE

¼ cup bottled hoisin sauce or teriyaki sauce or homemade Teriyaki Sauce (page 241)

2 tablespoons soy sauce

1 teaspoon sriracha or other hot sauce, or more to taste

1 teaspoon sesame oil

FOR THE CHOW MEIN

1 (8-ounce) package chow mein noodles (yakisoba; see note)

2 tablespoons safflower or other high-heat oil

1 medium onion, quartered and thinly sliced

8 ounces chicken-style plant protein (see options at left), cut into bite-size chunks or strips

1 red bell pepper, cut into narrow strips

3 large celery stalks, sliced on the diagonal

4 to 5 ounces shiitake or other brown mushrooms, cleaned, stemmed, and sliced

8 ounces fresh mung bean sprouts

1 cup thawed frozen green peas

3 to 4 scallions, thinly sliced

1 Combine the ingredients for the sauce in a small bowl. Stir and set aside.

2 Cook the noodles according to package directions until al dente, then drain. These noodles are very long, so reach into the colander and cut here and there with kitchen shears to shorten.

3 Meanwhile, heat the oil in a stir-fry pan. Add the onion and stir-fry over medium heat until translucent. Add the chick'n and continue to stir-fry until both it and the onion are golden brown, about 8 minutes.

4 Add the bell pepper, celery, and mushrooms and stir-fry over medium-high heat for a minute or two, until just crisp-tender.

5 Stir in the sprouts, peas, and scallions and continue to stir-fry just until heated through. Remove from the heat.

6 Add the cooked noodles and sauce to the vegetables and mix together with a large fork. Taste to see if you want to add any more of the sauce ingredients or pass extra soy sauce and hot sauce at the table.

ORANGE CHICK'N
& BROCCOLI

SERVES 4

QUICK AND COLORFUL, THIS dish gets its subtle fruity flavor from a splash of fresh orange juice and some preserves—orange or apricot. And if you're like me and tend to get lazy around 6:00 p.m., you can use a bottled Asian sauce such as teriyaki or kung pao instead of the homemade version. You can substitute whatever vegetables you may have on hand for those suggested in the recipe.

This dish is a nice way to highlight plant-based chicken strips, but it's also excellent when made with firm, chewy baked tofu.

PLANT PROTEIN OPTIONS

Plant-based chick'n strips or chunks

½ recipe Chicken-Style Seitan Cutlets (page 222)

Baked tofu

1 tablespoon safflower or other neutral vegetable oil

⅓ cup bottled teriyaki or kung pao sauce or homemade Teriyaki Sauce (page 241), divided

8 to 10 ounces chicken-style plant protein (see options at left), cut into bite-size strips or chunks

Juice of ½ orange

1 large or 2 medium broccoli crowns, cut into bite-size florets

4 or 5 stalks bok choy or 1 baby bok choy, sliced

1 medium red bell pepper, diced

2 to 3 scallions, cut into 1-inch lengths

⅓ cup orange or apricot preserves, preferably all-fruit

2 teaspoons grated fresh or squeeze-bottle ginger

Freshly ground pepper to taste

FOR SERVING (OPTIONAL)

Sriracha or other hot sauce to taste

Hot cooked rice or other grain

½ fresh orange, thinly sliced

Toasted cashews or peanuts

1 Heat the oil and 2 tablespoons of the teriyaki sauce in a skillet or stir-fry pan over medium-high heat. When it's sizzling hot, add the protein and stir-fry for 3 to 4 minutes.

2 Add the orange juice and broccoli and stir-fry for a minute or so. Then layer on the bok choy, bell pepper, and scallions, but don't stir yet.

3 In a small bowl, combine the remaining teriyaki sauce with the preserves and ginger and stir. Pour over the vegetables and give them a good toss.

4 Stir-fry just until the vegetables are crisp-tender—this won't take much longer, just a minute or so; make sure not to overcook!

5 Season with pepper and add hot sauce if desired (or just pass the sauce at the table). Serve the mixture on its own or over hot cooked grains. This makes a pretty bowl, garnished with thin slices of the remaining orange half and a sprinkling of toasted nuts.

PINEAPPLE
STIR-FRIED RICE

SERVES 6 TO 8

THIS THAI-INSPIRED PINEAPPLE STIR-FRIED rice treats the palate to occasional bursts of juicy sweetness and features two different kinds of protein. Chicken is the standard, and it's paired with either some sort of pork or shrimp. Variations are endless, but we'll go with plant-based chicken (or, just as good, baked tofu) and plant-based deli slices. If you want something a bit more exotic, use plant-based shrimp or seafood in place of either.

PLANT PROTEIN OPTIONS

Plant-based chick'n strips or chunks

½ recipe Chicken-Style Seitan Cutlets (page 222)

Baked tofu

VARIATION

Use brown rice in place of the rice-quinoa combination. Combine 1½ cups uncooked brown rice with 3½ cups water in a medium saucepan. Bring to a slow boil, then reduce the heat, cover, and cook until the water is absorbed, about 30 minutes. If you prefer a more tender grain, add ½ cup additional water and cook until absorbed.

1 cup uncooked long-grain white rice

½ cup uncooked quinoa, any color (red looks nice)

3 cups water, plus more if desired

2 tablespoons safflower or other high-heat oil

1 medium onion, finely chopped

1 bell pepper, any color, cut into short, thin slices

3 scallions, thinly sliced

8 ounces chicken-style plant protein (see options at left), cut into bite-size chunks

3 or 4 plant-based deli slices, any variety, cut into short, narrow strips

1 cup thawed frozen green peas

1 (16- to 20-ounce) can pineapple chunks in unsweetened juice, drained (reserve juice for another use)

2 tablespoons freshly squeezed lemon or lime juice

3 tablespoons soy sauce, or more to taste

Freshly ground pepper to taste

Lime wedges for garnish

1 Combine the rice and quinoa with the water in a medium saucepan. Bring to a slow boil, then lower the heat and cook, partially covered, for 15 minutes, or until the water is absorbed. If you prefer a more tender grain, add ½ cup additional water and cook until absorbed.

2 Meanwhile, heat the oil in a large skillet or stir-fry pan. Add the onion and sauté over medium heat until translucent. Add the bell pepper and continue to sauté until the onion is golden.

3 Add the scallions and chick'n or tofu and stir-fry 2 to 3 minutes over medium-high heat.

4 When the rice is done, add it to the pan. Stir-fry for another 2 to 3 minutes.

5 Add the remaining ingredients and continue to stir-fry for a few more minutes, until everything harmonizes nicely and is touched with golden brown here and there. Garnish with lime wedges and serve at once, straight from the pan.

PEPPER STEAK

SERVES 4 TO 6

HERE'S AN OLD-SCHOOL CLASSIC featuring bell peppers in several hues stir-fried with beefy plant protein. There are a number of plant-based meaty products that are packaged in strips, which is handy. Seitan is also an ideal protein for this dish—the kind you buy or, better yet, the kind you make. Vegetable spring rolls from the freezer section of your grocery are a fun side dish for this meal, along with orange slices.

PLANT PROTEIN OPTIONS

Plant-based beefy strips, chunks, or steak

Seitan

½ recipe Traditional Beef-Style Seitan (page 219)

2 tablespoons safflower or other neutral vegetable oil, divided

2 tablespoons soy sauce, divided

12 to 16 beef-style plant protein strips or chunks (see options at left), cut into bite-size pieces

1 large onion, quartered and thinly sliced

2 cloves garlic, minced

1 green bell pepper, cut into 2-inch strips

1 red bell pepper, cut into 2-inch strips

1 yellow or orange bell pepper, cut into 2-inch strips

¼ cup dry red wine or sherry (optional)

2 teaspoons grated fresh or squeeze-bottle ginger

1½ tablespoons cornstarch or arrowroot

½ cup water

Hot cooked rice or noodles for serving

2 scallions, thinly sliced, for garnish (optional)

1 Heat 1 tablespoon oil and 1 tablespoon soy sauce in a stir-fry pan over medium heat. Add the plant protein, stir quickly to coat, and increase the heat to medium-high. Stir-fry until lightly browned on most sides. Transfer to a plate until needed.

2 Heat the remaining oil in the same pan. Add the onion and sauté over medium heat until golden. Add the garlic and bell peppers, increase the heat, and stir-fry until the peppers are crisp-tender, about 3 minutes.

3 Stir in the remaining soy sauce, wine if desired, and ginger.

4 In a small bowl, dissolve the cornstarch in just enough of the water to make it smooth and pourable, then add the remaining water. Stir again, drizzle into the pan, and cook until thickened. Serve at once over hot cooked rice or noodles, garnished with scallions if desired.

MONGOLIAN-ISH BEEF

SERVES 4

I WAS CURIOUS WHETHER the dish known as Mongolian beef has anything to do with Mongolia or its cuisine. Not surprisingly, it doesn't. Like chop suey, it seems to be a Western invention. What is it about that sweet and savory sauce that appeals so to the American palate? Could it be the full cup of sugar used in standard recipes to make the sauce? Yes, that's a serious amount of sugar in a beefy dish! I've replaced the sugar with apricot preserves, which adds a subtly sweet flavor that enhances rather than drowns the dish. Mongolian beef is often served without any vegetable other than bell peppers and scallions—a wasted opportunity! I've opted to use asparagus, but feel free to use any other green vegetable or two, including broccoli, bok choy, and green beans.

PLANT PROTEIN OPTIONS

Plant-based beefy strips or steak

Seitan

½ recipe Traditional Beef-Style Seitan (page 219)

12 to 16 ounces beef-style plant protein (see options at left), cut into bite-size strips

2 tablespoons cornstarch or arrowroot

⅓ cup bottled teriyaki sauce or homemade Teriyaki Sauce (page 241)

⅓ cup all-fruit apricot preserves

2 teaspoons minced fresh or squeeze-bottle ginger

3 tablespoons safflower or other neutral vegetable oil, divided

3 to 4 cloves garlic, minced

10 to 12 stalks asparagus, trimmed and cut into 2-inch lengths

½ red or orange bell pepper, cut into short, thin strips

3 to 4 scallions, thinly sliced, divided

Hot cooked rice for serving

1. Sprinkle the plant protein with the cornstarch and stir to distribute.

2. Combine the teriyaki sauce, preserves, and ginger in a small bowl and whisk.

3. Heat about half the oil in a skillet or stir-fry pan. When sizzling hot, add the beefy strips and stir-fry over high heat for 8 minutes or so, until golden brown on most sides.

4. Stir in half the teriyaki mixture and continue to stir-fry for just a minute or so longer, until nicely glazed. Transfer to a plate or bowl.

5. Wipe out the pan, then heat the remaining oil. Add the garlic and sauté over low heat for a minute or so.

6. Add the asparagus and a little water, just enough to keep the bottom of the pan moist. Turn the heat back up and stir-fry until the asparagus is bright green and crisp-tender, just a minute or two.

7. Add the plant protein along with the bell pepper and about half the scallions. Continue to stir-fry briefly, just until everything is sizzling hot.

8. Serve over or alongside hot cooked rice. Garnish individual servings with the remaining scallions.

THAI COCONUT CURRY MEATBALLS

SERVES 6

THIS SAUCY THAI-STYLE DISH is more of a homey meal than something you'd find on a take-out menu, but even so, it seems like a perfect fit for this chapter. As always, when a dish requires a curry backdrop, I rely on ready-made Indian simmer sauces, since these miracles in a jar do a much better job of creating amazingly complex flavors than I ever could. Here, as in this recipe's traditional counterpart, a generous amount of rich coconut curry envelops hearty meatballs. Have some rice or quinoa ready to absorb that delectable sauce.

NOTE: *For this dish choose a dairy-free variety of Indian simmer sauce, such as jalfrezi or rogan josh for a mild flavor. The Madras curry variety is also usually dairy-free, and that's an ideal choice if you want a spicier effect.*

FOR THE COCONUT CURRY SAUCE
1 cup Indian simmer sauce (see note)

1 cup light coconut milk

¼ cup natural smooth peanut butter

2 teaspoons grated fresh or squeeze-bottle ginger

1 teaspoon sriracha or Thai red curry paste, plus more for serving

Juice of ½ lime

FOR THE MEATBALLS
2 tablespoons safflower or other neutral vegetable oil, divided

1 (12- to 16-ounce) package plant-based meatballs or Teriyaki Meatballs (page 218)

1 medium onion, quartered and thinly sliced

1 medium red bell pepper, cut into long, narrow pieces

FOR SERVING
Fresh cilantro leaves

1 cup fresh mung bean sprouts (optional)

Hot cooked rice or quinoa

Lime wedges (optional)

1 Combine the sauce ingredients in a mixing bowl and whisk.

2 Heat 1 tablespoon oil in a wide skillet. Add the meatballs and sauté over medium heat, turning occasionally, until most sides are crisp and golden-brown, 8 to 10 minutes. Transfer to a plate or bowl.

3 Heat the remaining oil in the same skillet. Add the onion and sauté over medium heat until translucent. Add the bell pepper and continue to sauté until both are golden.

4 Pour the sauce into the skillet and let it come to a simmer. Add the meatballs to the skillet and cook over low heat for a few minutes longer, until the sauce thickens around them.

5 Scatter the cilantro and bean sprouts, if desired, over the meatballs and sauce. Serve at once over hot cooked grains and garnish with lime wedges, if desired. Pass extra hot sauce at the table.

SPICY UDON STIR-FRY
WITH GROUND & CABBAGE

SERVES 4

IN ITS ORIGINAL FORM, this recipe uses ground pork. Here you can start with beefy plant-based ground, go straight to plant-based chorizo, or make your own Tempeh and Mushroom Chorizo (page 215). Whichever you opt for, the spicy "meat" mingling with thick udon noodles and plenty of cabbage makes for an easy, hearty dish with plenty of personality.

PLANT PROTEIN OPTIONS

Plant-based chorizo (if using this, you may want to taste before adding sriracha, because some varieties can be spicy)

Plant-based ground

1 recipe Tempeh and Mushroom Chorizo (page 215)

1 (8-ounce) package udon noodles or 8 ounces linguine

2 tablespoons safflower or other neutral vegetable oil, divided

5 cups coarsely chopped green cabbage

2 to 3 cloves garlic, minced

10 to 12 ounces plant-based ground (see options at left)

¼ cup good-quality natural ketchup

2 teaspoons sriracha or other hot sauce, or more to taste

2 teaspoons smoked paprika or barbecue seasoning

¼ cup bottled teriyaki sauce or homemade Teriyaki Sauce (page 241), or more to taste, divided

2 teaspoons grated fresh or squeeze-bottle ginger

4 to 5 scallions, thinly sliced, divided

Crushed peanuts or sesame seeds for topping

1 Cook the noodles according to package directions until al dente, then drain.

2 Meanwhile, heat 1 tablespoon oil in a stir-fry pan. Add the cabbage and garlic and stir-fry over high heat until the cabbage is crisp-tender and just starting to be touched with brown spots, about 5 minutes. Transfer to a bowl.

3 Reduce the heat to medium-high and add the remaining oil to the pan. Add the ground (break up with a spatula if clumpy), ketchup, sriracha, paprika, and about 1 tablespoon of the teriyaki sauce.

4 Stir over medium-high heat until well blended. Let cook undisturbed for a minute or two, until the underside is browned, then turn the mixture over with a spatula and let the underside brown again. Break up the mixture again if necessary.

5 Add the cooked noodles, ginger, remaining teriyaki sauce, and a bit more than half the scallions to the pan. Use a large fork to distribute the spicy ground through the noodles while stir-frying over medium-high heat for 2 to 3 minutes.

6 Serve straight from the pan, topping each serving with crushed peanuts or sesame seeds.

THAI PEANUT
BUDDHA BOWLS

SERVES 2

THIS RECIPE IS LESS characteristic of take-out menu offerings and more of a way to use leftover ingredients you might have lurking in the fridge. Yet the results can be nothing short of spectacular. If you're someone who enjoys Asian flavors as much as I do, you'll find this a treat for both the eyes and the palate.

The plant protein options are flexible; the bed of grains or noodles even more so. The point is to use what you've got on hand—and be generous with the peanut sauce. Don't hesitate to double the recipe if there are more than two of you at the table.

GRAIN & NOODLE OPTIONS

White or brown rice

Quinoa

Bean threads

Udon or soba noodles

Spaghetti or angel hair pasta

PLANT PROTEIN OPTIONS

Chicken-style plant protein

Seitan

½ recipe Traditional Beef-Style Seitan (page 219)

Tempeh

Baked tofu

1 cup bite-size broccoli florets

2 teaspoons safflower or other neutral vegetable oil

8 to 10 ounces plant-based protein (see options at left)

⅓ cup Coconut Peanut Sauce (page 236) or bottled peanut satay sauce, plus more for serving

2 cups hot cooked grains or noodles (see options at left)

½ cup thinly sliced red or green cabbage

½ cup grated carrot

Fresh mung bean sprouts or other green sprouts, such as radish sprouts or pea shoots

GARNISHES

Lime wedges

Fresh cilantro leaves

Chopped peanuts

1. In a medium skillet, combine the broccoli with just enough water to keep the pan moist. Cover and steam just until the broccoli is bright green, 2 to 3 minutes, then drain and rinse with cool water until the florets stop steaming.

2. Heat the oil in the same skillet. Add the plant protein of your choice and sauté over medium-high heat until golden on most sides, stirring often. Pour in the peanut sauce and continue to cook for just a couple of minutes longer, until the protein is nicely enveloped by the sauce.

3. To serve, divide the grains or noodles between two wide shallow bowls. Arrange half the protein more or less in the center of each bowl. Surround it with separate mounds of broccoli, cabbage, carrots, and sprouts.

4. Garnish the bowls with lime wedges, cilantro, and chopped peanuts and serve at once. Pass the remaining peanut sauce at the table.

KOREAN BEEFY BOWLS

SERVES 4

A KOREAN BEEF BOWL is a simple dish made of ground beef bathed in a gently spiced and slightly sweet sauce, served over rice and topped with scallions. A seriously easy dish to convert to plant-based, it's quick enough to make as a weeknight meal. If you have a little more time, this is an ideal dish for using Teriyaki-Flavored Ground (page 218), made with black beans, red quinoa, and walnuts, which is quick to prepare. Alongside the fresh vegetables, kimchi is a fitting addition to the meal. If you decide to use it, make sure you get a vegan variety, because some varieties contain fish.

Look for Korean barbecue sauce in the Asian foods section of well-stocked supermarkets. If it's unavailable, bottled or homemade teriyaki sauce is a fine substitute.

PLANT PROTEIN OPTIONS

Beef-style ground or crumbles

4 beef-style vegan burgers, crumbled

1 tablespoon safflower or other neutral vegetable oil

2 to 3 cloves garlic, minced

1 recipe Teriyaki-Flavored Ground (page 218) or 11 to 14 ounces packaged plant-based beef-style ground or crumbles (see options at left)

½ cup bottled Korean barbecue sauce or homemade Teriyaki Sauce (page 241), plus more to taste

3½ to 4 cups hot cooked rice or other grains

2 scallions, thinly sliced

Sliced fresh vegetables such as cucumber, bell peppers, avocado, and/or radishes for topping

Kimchi to taste (optional)

FOR THE SRIRACHA MAYONNAISE (OPTIONAL)

½ cup vegan mayonnaise

2 teaspoons sriracha or other hot sauce, or to taste

1 **If using packaged plant-based beef-style ground:** Heat the oil in a medium skillet. Add the garlic and sauté over low heat for a minute or two. Add the beef-style ground and the barbecue sauce and cook over medium-high heat until sizzling hot and starting to brown. Taste and add more sauce if desired.

2 **If using Teriyaki-Flavored Ground:** Omit the oil, garlic, and barbecue sauce, and skip step 1.

3 **If using sriracha mayonnaise:** Combine the mayonnaise and sriracha in a small bowl, stir, and set aside to let the flavors meld.

4 Distribute the rice among four shallow bowls.

5 Distribute the prepared ground over the rice. Sprinkle the scallions on top, leaving room for the fresh vegetables.

6 Arrange the fresh vegetables and kimchi, if using, on the side of each bowl. Serve immediately, passing the sriracha mayonnaise at the table if desired.

KOREAN BULGOGI BOWLS

SERVES 2

KOREAN BULGOGI IS A kind of cousin to Korean Beefy Bowls (page 114) and other ground beef–style dishes. In this variation, the beefy plant protein is in strips or chunks rather than ground. Bulgogi bowls are generously embellished with raw vegetables—typically cucumbers, carrots, and radishes. The finished dish is served with sriracha mayonnaise, which adds another level of luscious flavor. Like the Thai Peanut Buddha Bowls (page 113), this recipe doubles easily.

PLANT PROTEIN OPTIONS

Plant-based beefy tips or strips

Seitan

½ recipe Traditional Beef-Style Seitan (page 219)

FOR THE SRIRACHA MAYONNAISE
½ cup vegan mayonnaise

2 teaspoons sriracha or other hot sauce, or to taste

FOR THE BULGOGI
2 teaspoons safflower or other neutral vegetable oil

8 ounces beef-style plant protein (see options at left), cut into bite-size pieces or strips

¼ cup bottled Korean barbecue sauce or homemade Teriyaki Sauce (page 241), or more to taste

2 cups hot cooked rice

12 thin slices cucumber

⅓ cup grated carrots or quartered baby carrots

4 radishes, thinly sliced

GARNISHES
1 scallion, thinly sliced

Fresh mint or basil leaves

1 Combine the mayonnaise and sriracha in a small bowl, stir, and set aside.

2 Heat the oil in a medium skillet. Add the plant protein and sauté over medium heat until lightly browned on most sides, about 8 minutes. Stir in the barbecue sauce and cook for a minute or two longer.

3 Divide the rice between two wide shallow bowls. Divide the protein between them, spooning it on one side. Arrange a row of cucumber slices, carrots, and radishes next to the protein.

4 Sprinkle with one or both of the garnishes, then serve. Pass the sriracha mayo at the table.

**Korean Beefy Bowls,
page 114**

CHAPTER 5
SANDWICHES & SUCH

SANDWICHES HAVE LONG BEEN one of the cornerstones of meaty fare. Now the plant-based world has appropriated many of these classic recipes. Like all vegan preparations, both in this book and in the world at large, meaty sandwiches of the plant-based variety are lower in fat than their traditional versions and free of cholesterol. We'll be sneaking in more vegetables, too. I've always maintained, for example, that wraps are really salads in disguise.

I have to admit that I rebel a bit at following specific recipes for sandwiches and wraps and using exact quantities for burger and pizza embellishments. In some instances, general guidelines are helpful, but feel free to take liberties, just as I've done to create the plant-strong versions of classic sandwiches. Use any recipe as a springboard for your own ideas. It comes down to this: choose some bread or bready item (such as a wrap, pizza crust, bun, or roll), then pile on the protein, vegetables, and condiments. You don't have to be exact—nothing can go wrong!

GYROS

GYROS, THE GREEK PITA wraps, are so easy to convert to vegan with most any kind of beef-style plant protein chunks. Seitan works quite well, too. To save some time and effort, a ready-made vegan ranch or creamy dill dressing can be used to fast-track a tasty tzatziki-style sauce. Or you can take a few extra moments to make my tasty bean-based Vegan Ranch Dressing (page 238).

PLANT PROTEIN OPTIONS

Plant-based beefy tips or strips

Seitan

⅓ recipe Traditional Beef-Style Seitan (page 219)

TIPS

Gyros always seem to want to tear open at the bottom, so the sandwich is often wrapped in foil. You can peel it away as you eat.

Even though it's traditional to wrap an intact pita around the filling, you can cut an opening in the pita and fill the resulting pocket for a less authentic (but also less messy) experience.

1½ tablespoons extra-virgin olive oil

1 medium onion, finely chopped

2 cloves garlic, minced

8 to 10 ounces beef-style plant protein (see options at left)

½ teaspoon dried oregano

½ teaspoon ground cumin

½ cucumber, peeled

⅓ cup bottled vegan ranch dressing or homemade Vegan Ranch Dressing (page 238), plus more to taste

4 pitas, preferably whole-grain, regular or pocketless

Thinly shredded dark green lettuce to taste

2 ripe fresh plum (Roma) tomatoes, thinly sliced, or more to taste

1 Heat the oil in a medium skillet. Add the onion and sauté over medium-low heat until translucent. Add the garlic and continue to sauté until both are just beginning to turn golden.

2 Add the plant protein, oregano, and cumin. Increase the heat and continue to sauté until golden and crisp on most sides, 6 to 8 minutes, then remove from the heat.

3 Quarter the cucumber lengthwise, remove the seeds if they appear watery, and slice. In a small bowl, combine the cucumber with the dressing and stir.

4 To assemble, place a pita on each individual serving plate. Arrange a little lettuce over the surface of each, followed by the protein, then the cucumber mixture. Arrange three slices or so of tomato down the center of each. Fold the pitas around the filling and eat out of hand.

PHILLY CHEESESTEAKS
WITH PORTOBELLOS

MAKES 4 CHEESESTEAKS

WHEN IT COMES TO veganizing the iconic Philly cheesesteak, all it takes is one-to-one swaps with plant protein (beef-style, usually) and vegan cheese. Some vegan versions of cheesesteak use portobello mushrooms only, which, despite their meaty umami, aren't a good source of protein. Combining beefy plant protein and portobellos creates a perfect balance of textures and flavors. This fuss-free preparation can be eaten by itself or served alongside a bountiful salad for a filling dinner.

1 tablespoon extra-virgin olive oil

1 large onion, quartered and thinly sliced

1 medium bell pepper, any color, cut into strips

8 to 10 ounces beefy plant protein or seitan, cut into strips

2 portobello mushrooms, stemmed, cleaned, halved, and thinly sliced

1½ cups vegan mozzarella-style cheese shreds

4 hero rolls (preferably whole-grain)

Hot seasoning such as sriracha, hot pepper sauce, or dried hot red pepper flakes to taste

1 Heat the oil in a wide skillet. Add the onion and sauté over medium heat until translucent.

2 Add the bell pepper, beefy strips, and mushrooms. Increase the heat to medium-high and continue to sauté, stirring often, until the mixture is touched with brown spots, 6 to 8 minutes.

3 Scatter the cheese evenly over the mixture in the pan. Reduce the heat to medium and cover; cook just until the cheese melts, 2 to 3 minutes.

4 Scooping from the bottom, distribute the filling evenly over the bottom halves of the hero rolls (if you want, you can hollow them out a bit so that more of the filling can go in). This will fill four or more hero rolls, depending on their size.

5 Let everyone top with hot sauce or red pepper flakes as desired. Serve open-faced or cover with the top halves of the rolls.

BARBECUE-FLAVORED CHICK'N MELT BAGUETTES

MAKES 4 MELTS

HERE'S AN EASY, BIG sandwich to make with chicken-style plant protein, a flavorful barbecue sauce, fresh bread, and melted vegan cheese. This works well with any of the various forms of plant-based chicken—breaded nuggets, scallopine, or strips. And, of course, when you have more time and the inclination, you can make your own Chicken-Style Seitan Cutlets (page 222), which are absolutely perfect for this.

PLANT PROTEIN OPTIONS

Plant-based chick'n strips

½ recipe Chicken-Style Seitan Cutlets (page 222)

Baked tofu

Tempeh

1 tablespoon extra-virgin olive oil

1 large or 2 medium onions, quartered and thinly sliced

8 to 10 ounces plant-based chicken (see options at left), cut into narrow strips

½ cup bottled barbecue sauce or Quick No-Cook Barbecue Sauce (page 240), or more to taste

1 whole-grain baguette or Italian bread loaf, preferably not too narrow

½ to 1 cup vegan mozzarella-style cheese shreds

TOPPINGS (CHOOSE ONE OR MORE)

1 jalapeño pepper, sliced

¼ cup coarsely chopped fresh cilantro or parsley leaves

1 scallion, green part only, thinly sliced

1 Preheat the oven to 400°F. Line a baking sheet with parchment paper.

2 Heat the oil in a medium skillet. Add the onions and sauté over medium heat until soft and starting to turn golden, about 8 minutes.

3 Add the plant protein and continue to sauté until the onions are touched with brown, about 5 minutes. Stir in the barbecue sauce and continue to cook for 5 minutes longer, or until the sauce envelops the protein and onions nicely. Stir in a little more sauce if desired.

4 Cut the baguette in half horizontally, then cut each section in half lengthwise. Scoop some of the bread from each of the quarters to create hollows (reserve the extra bread for another use, such as making bread crumbs).

Recipe continues

5 Distribute the protein mixture among the four hollowed-out baguette sections. How much you'll use depends on the size of the bread and how much you've hollowed out. If you wind up with a little excess protein, it's tasty to eat on its own or in a salad.

6 Top the protein mixture with the cheese shreds, generously or lightly as you prefer. If you choose jalapeño as a topping, scatter it here and there over the cheese. If you choose scallions and/or cilantro leaves, wait until the baguettes are out of the oven to scatter them over the cheese.

7 Bake on the prepared baking sheet for 5 to 8 minutes, or until the cheese is nicely melted. Each section of the baguette constitutes one serving, but if they're part of a larger meal, you can cut each section in half again to create more servings.

EASY PINEAPPLE COLESLAW

SERVES 4 AS A SIDE DISH OR 6 AS A SANDWICH TOPPING

A couple of recipes in this chapter call for pineapple coleslaw to be layered onto a sandwich or wrap. This subtle slaw provides a refreshing contrast to highly flavored plant-based meats, especially those mixed with barbecue and jerk sauces. This recipe makes more than you'll need for most sandwiches, but no matter—it's good to eat on its own. If you want an even larger quantity to serve as a salad, it's easy to double the recipe.

2 cups thinly shredded cabbage or bagged coleslaw

½ cup well drained canned crushed pineapple

½ medium red bell pepper, finely diced (optional)

¼ cup vegan mayonnaise

Chopped fresh cilantro to taste

1 tablespoon freshly squeezed lemon or lime juice

Freshly ground pepper to taste

Combine all ingredients in a mixing bowl and stir. Let stand for 10 minutes or so, if time allows, to let the flavors blend and allow the cabbage to soften.

JERK CHICK'N
WRAPS

MAKES 2 WRAPS

MUCH AS I LIKE a good shortcut, I haven't yet found a bottled jerk sauce I love. I hope you'll want to use the easy, if perhaps not entirely authentic, homemade Jerk Sauce on page 237. If you have a favorite prepared jerk sauce, though, by all means use it.

The savory and spicy chick'n contrasts beautifully with the slightly sweet coleslaw in these generous wraps. For an easy meal, accompany the wraps with baked or microwaved sweet potatoes. The salad portion of your meal is in the wrap itself!

PLANT PROTEIN OPTIONS

Plant-based chicken, any variety

½ recipe Chicken-Style Seitan Cutlets (page 222)

Baked tofu

2 teaspoons extra-virgin olive oil

7 to 8 ounces chicken-style plant protein (see options at left)

⅓ to ½ cup Jerk Sauce (page 237) or good-quality bottled jerk sauce

2 (10-inch) wraps

Vegan mayonnaise to taste

½ recipe Easy Pineapple Coleslaw (page 126)

½ small jalapeño pepper, seeded and sliced (optional)

1 Heat the oil in a medium skillet. Add the protein and sauté over medium-high heat, stirring frequently, until golden brown on most sides.

2 Reduce the heat to medium. Add ⅓ cup jerk sauce and continue to cook for a minute or two, until the sauce envelops the protein nicely. Drizzle in a bit more if desired—this should be saucy but not soupy. Be a bit more cautious with bottled sauce, since it tends to be much saltier than homemade.

3 Lay the wraps on individual serving plates or a cutting board. Spread a small amount of mayonnaise over most of the surface of each wrap (this will help keep them together). Divide the coleslaw between the wraps, arranging it in a mound in the center. Arrange the chick'n strips over it and top with the jalapeño slices, if desired.

4 Fold two ends of each wrap over, then roll up snugly in the opposite direction, making sure the ends stay tucked in. Cut each wrap in half and serve at once.

REUBENESQUE
SANDWICHES

MAKES 4 OPEN-FACED SANDWICHES

THE CLASSIC REUBEN SANDWICH is easy to make meatless as well as dairy-free. It's great for a quick at-home lunch or for a soup-and-sandwich dinner. This interpretation takes lots of culinary license with the original, but the contrasting flavors are all there, including the must-have sauerkraut. Try to use a real fermented sauerkraut, which is as good for your gut as it is for your palate.

VARIATIONS

Substitute plant-based deli slices, plant-based beef, or seitan strips for the bacon.

Step up the flavor and heat by using a spicy cabbage kimchi in place of the sauerkraut.

FOR THE THOUSAND ISLAND-ISH DRESSING

½ cup vegan mayonnaise

¼ cup good-quality natural ketchup

1 tablespoon organic sweet pickle relish

FOR THE SANDWICHES

1 tablespoon vegan butter or olive oil, plus more for the pan

8 ounces plant-based bacon or Smoky Tempeh Strips (page 224)

4 slices whole-grain bread

4 vegan cheese slices, any style

1 medium ripe avocado, pitted, peeled, and thinly sliced

2 medium ripe fresh tomatoes, thinly sliced

Well-drained sauerkraut to taste

1 Combine the ingredients for the dressing in a small bowl and stir until smooth.

2 Heat the vegan butter or olive oil in a wide skillet over medium heat. Add the bacon and cook until lightly browned on both sides, 6 to 8 minutes total. (Alternatively, prepare the Smoky Tempeh Strips as directed in the recipe.) Transfer to a plate and cover.

3 Wipe the skillet fairly clean and heat with just enough additional vegan butter or olive oil to coat the surface once again.

4 Arrange the bread slices in the skillet (cook in two batches if they don't fit). Cover each with a slice of cheese, then layer the remaining ingredients as follows: avocado slices, tomato slices, cooked bacon, and as much or as little sauerkraut as you like.

5 Heat the sandwiches over medium heat until the cheese melts. Serve at once, open-faced.

BIG
ROAST BEEFY
SANDWICHES

MAKES 2 SANDWICHES

THICK, SLICEABLE PLANT-BASED ROAST beef is one of the newest forms of plant-based protein, but I have a feeling it will continue to become more widely available. If you can't find this product, beef-style deli slices will do just fine—or really any variety of deli slices you find or have on hand. Prepared or homemade pesto, roasted red pepper, and cucumber join forces to create a delicious array of flavors to enhance this big sandwich.

If making your own pesto, do so first. You won't need the entire recipe for these two big sandwiches, but you might as well make the entire quantity in case you want to use it in future sandwiches—or on pasta or as a salad dressing.

½ cup Very Green Pesto (page 244) or prepared vegan pesto, or more to taste

2 kaiser or other sandwich rolls, preferably whole-grain

1 roasted red pepper, drained, very well blotted, and cut into narrow strips

6 to 8 slices roast beef–style plant protein, warmed if desired

12 or so very thin cucumber slices or 1 medium ripe fresh tomato, thinly sliced

Prepared yellow or Dijon mustard to taste

1 Spread a generous layer of pesto on the bottom half of a roll. Follow with half the roasted pepper, a few slices of plant-based roast beef, and cucumber. Top with a little more pesto. Spread mustard on the top half of the roll and cover the sandwich.

2 Repeat with the second roll, then serve at once.

TURK'Y
WRAPS
WITH ARUGULA, APPLE & AVOCADO

MAKES 2 WRAPS

ADDING APPLE SLICES TO wraps results in an unexpected pop of juicy sweetness. Combine them with plant-based deli slices, peppery arugula, and mellow avocado, and you have a delectable wrap that takes just minutes to prepare. Enjoy it for a tasty lunch at home, or pack it for work or school. These wraps also make a quick dinner when served with a simple potato or sweet potato dish.

2 (10-inch) wraps

¼ cup Tartar Sauce (page 239) or vegan mayonnaise, or more to taste

8 turkey-style plant-based deli slices

½ crisp sweet apple, thinly sliced

½ small or ¼ medium ripe avocado, pitted, peeled, and thinly sliced, or more to taste

Baby arugula to taste

1 Lay a wrap on a plate or cutting board. Spread the surface generously with half the tartar sauce.

2 Arrange 4 overlapping deli slices down the center, leaving some room on either end. Arrange half the apples in a row over the deli slices, and next to the apple, a row of half the avocado. Top with some baby arugula—a couple of big handfuls should do.

3 Fold two sides of the wrap over the ingredients, then roll up snugly, making sure the sides stay tucked in. Cut in half with a sharp knife.

4 Repeat with the second wrap and serve.

"TUNA" HUMMUS WRAPS

WITH AVOCADO, TOMATO & OLIVES

MAKES 2 WRAPS

THIS RECIPE MIGHT AS well be called "every yummy sandwich ingredient, all wrapped together." Hummus and avocado, two fantastic wrap ingredients, become even more delectable with the addition of plant-based tuna. And of course you're always free to use baked tofu if that's your preference. This is a fantastic lunch to take to school or work or serve for dinner with a simple soup or potato dish.

VARIATIONS

Substitute 6 to 8 ounces of crumbled baked tofu or 1 recipe Crazy Easy Chickpea Chick'n (page 225) for the tuna. To give these a mildly fishy flavor, mix in ½ teaspoon of dulse flakes (a dried seaweed used as seasoning) with the protein.

2 (10- to 12-inch) wraps, preferably whole-grain

⅓ cup prepared or homemade hummus, or more to taste

3 to 4 ounces plant-based tuna, flaked

1 medium ripe fresh tomato, thinly sliced

12 or so thin cucumber slices or a handful of green sprouts

½ medium ripe avocado, pitted, peeled, and sliced

¼ cup pitted and sliced brine-cured black olives

2 big handfuls baby greens, such as spinach, arugula, or power greens (see page 56)

1 Lay a wrap on a large plate or cutting board. Spread the hummus over the surface.

2 Arrange a row of the protein down the center of the wrap. On either side of it, place a few slices of tomato, avocado, and cucumber. Scatter the olives over the surface, then add a handful of greens.

3 Fold two sides of the wrap over the filling ingredients, then roll up snugly in the opposite direction, making sure the sides stay tucked in. Cut in half with a sharp knife.

4 Repeat with the second wrap and serve at once.

"TUNA" MELTS

A TUNA MELT IS a classic sandwich that's crazy easy to veganize. Mash (or flake) your protein of choice, slather with vegan mayo and a few extra embellishments, top with vegan cheese, and you've got a lively lunch. There's no reason this couldn't be a quick dinner as well, served with any kind of vegetable soup.

VARIATIONS

Substitute 6 to 8 ounces of crumbled baked tofu or 1 recipe Crazy Easy Chickpea Chick'n (page 225) for the tuna. To give these a mildly fishy flavor, mix in ½ teaspoon of dulse flakes (a dried seaweed used as seasoning) with the protein.

6 to 8 ounces plant-based tuna, flaked (see note)

⅓ cup vegan mayonnaise, or more to taste

2 medium celery stalks, finely diced

2 teaspoons organic sweet pickle relish (optional but highly recommended)

2 tablespoons minced fresh chives or scallions (optional)

6 slices whole-grain bread or 4 English muffins, split

Finely shredded lettuce or baby spinach to taste

Thinly sliced ripe fresh tomatoes to taste

1 cup vegan cheese shreds, any style, or more, as desired

1 Combine the plant-based tuna, mayonnaise, celery, relish (if desired), and chives in a mixing bowl and stir until well blended.

2 Toast the bread or muffins. Top with lettuce and tomatoes, then distribute the tuna mixture evenly over them.

3 Sprinkle with the vegan cheese and arrange on a platter. Microwave briefly or toast in a toaster oven just until the cheese is slightly melted—you don't want the other ingredients to get too warm or mushy. Serve at once.

NOTE: *Some plant-based tuna comes nicely flaked in the package, but if the kind you're using doesn't, simply flake with a fork.*

TRIPLE-BARBECUE
PULLED JACKFRUIT
& PROTEIN
SANDWICHES

MAKES 6 SANDWICHES

JACKFRUIT IS OFTEN USED as an alternative to pulled pork, and any product that takes the place of meat is a good thing in my book. But in and of itself, jackfruit isn't a good protein source. Even an average serving of broccoli has about 4 grams of protein, whereas a serving of jackfruit has about 2 grams.

For extra protein and heartiness, this recipe pairs jackfruit with plant protein cut into short narrow pieces or shreds to more or less match the jackfruit's texture. The triple barbecue flavoring comes from the seasonings added to packaged jackfruit, your favorite barbecue sauce, and barbecue seasoning.

Like some of the other recipes in this chapter, this one includes a simple slaw with a little added pineapple, which contrasts nicely with the barbecue flavors. Don't worry if you have too much of it; you can always serve it the next day as a side salad.

PLANT PROTEIN OPTIONS

Plant-based chick'n

Seitan

Baked tofu

6 to 8 ounces plant protein (see options at left)

1 (10-ounce) package barbecue-flavored jackfruit

½ cup barbecue sauce

2 teaspoons barbecue seasoning

6 whole-grain rolls or hamburger buns

Easy Pineapple Coleslaw (page 126)

1 Cut the protein into short, narrow shreds or run it through the grating blade of a food processor. If you're using a firm variety of baked tofu, grate it with a box grater. You may also want to break up pieces of the jackfruit that are in large clumps; lightly mash with a fork, and it will flake nicely.

2 Combine the shredded plant protein, jackfruit, barbecue sauce, and barbecue seasoning in a medium skillet. Cook over medium heat for 8 to 10 minutes, or until the sauce envelops the mixture nicely and is sizzling hot.

3 Distribute the jackfruit mixture over the bottom halves of the rolls, then distribute the coleslaw evenly over it. Cover with the tops of the rolls and serve at once.

OPEN-FACED
CUBAN
SANDWICHES

MAKES 4 OPEN-FACED
SANDWICHES

THE CLASSIC CUBAN SANDWICH combines two kinds of pork—pulled and sliced—with cheese and pickles in one large, messy sandwich—a veritable feast of cholesterol! This one does away with the cholesterol; it's easy to swap pulled plant protein and vegan deli slices and cheese for the traditional ingredients.

It does retain its messy goodness, though, and that's why I opted to make these sandwiches open-faced. It's easier to eat them with a fork and knife than it is to pick them up and risk the components falling into your lap. Since the pulled plant protein is prepared with orange juice, get another orange or two to slice and serve as an accompaniment to this sandwich.

NOTE: *For these open-faced sandwiches, you'll need extra-large bread slices, not your standard slices. The center slices of fresh rye or sourdough bread loaves are ideal.*

FOR THE PULLED PROTEIN
1 tablespoon extra-virgin olive oil

8 to 10 ounces packaged barbecue-flavored plant-based pulled protein

1 teaspoon ground cumin

1 teaspoon dried oregano

Juice of ½ lime

Juice of ½ orange

FOR THE SANDWICHES
4 large slices whole-grain bread (see note)

Prepared yellow mustard to taste

8 Swiss- or pepper Jack–style vegan cheese slices, or more to taste

12 plant-based deli slices, preferably ham-style

Sliced pickles, preferably bread-and-butter, to taste

Extra-virgin olive oil or vegan butter for the pan

1 To make the protein, heat the oil in a wide skillet. Add the pulled protein and sauté over medium-high heat until piping hot.

2 Sprinkle in the cumin and oregano, then add the juices. Cook over medium-high heat, stirring often, until the pulled protein is nicely glazed, 5 to 7 minutes. Remove from the heat.

3 To assemble the sandwiches, spread each slice of bread with mustard. Top with 2 overlapping slices of cheese, 3 deli slices, the pulled protein, and finally a layer of sliced pickles.

4 Wipe the skillet out completely, then heat a little olive oil or butter just to coat the surface. Grill each sandwich over medium-high heat on one side only, covered, until the bread is golden and crusty and the cheese is melted. Cut each in half, then eat with fork and knife.

CLASSIC MEATY PIZZA
WITH ROASTED VEGETABLES

**MAKES 1 PIZZA,
6 SLICES**

DID YOU KNOW THAT pepperoni is the most popular pizza topping, followed by sausage, mushrooms, and bacon? Just think of how much we can do for the greater good by replacing these meats with their plant-based counterparts. Since plant pepperoni and plant sausage taste fairly similar when used as pizza toppings, you can choose one or the other for this pizza.

20 to 22 slices vegan pepperoni or 2 links vegan sausage, very thinly sliced

5 or 6 slices vegan bacon, cut into bits

2 cups finely chopped broccoli florets

1 cup brown mushrooms, cleaned, stemmed, and sliced, or 1 medium bell pepper, any color, cut into short, narrow strips

½ medium yellow onion, thinly sliced

1½ tablespoons extra-virgin olive oil

1 (12- to 14-inch) good-quality prepared pizza crust

1 cup good-quality pizza or marinara sauce, or to taste

1 to 1½ cups vegan mozzarella-style cheese shreds

TOPPINGS (OPTIONAL)
Baby spinach or other baby greens

Fresh oregano leaves or a few thinly sliced fresh basil leaves

Dried hot red pepper flakes

1 Preheat the oven to 425°F.

2 In a large mixing bowl, combine the pepperoni and bacon with the broccoli, mushrooms, and onion. Drizzle in the oil and stir. Transfer to a lightly oiled roasting pan and bake for 10 minutes.

3 Meanwhile, arrange the crust on a pizza stone or baking sheet. Distribute the sauce over the surface and sprinkle with the cheese. How much you use will depend on the size of the crust— and how cheesy you like your pizza. No need to measure these ingredients precisely.

4 Once the protein mixture has baked for 10 minutes, remove it from the oven and evenly distribute it over the surface of the pizza.

5 Bake the pizza for 12 minutes, or until the vegetables are lightly browned, the crust is golden, and the cheese is melted.

6 If you plan to use the spinach, scatter it over the surface of the pizza for just the last minute or two of baking.

7 Sprinkle the pizza with fresh herbs and/or red pepper flakes, if desired. Cut into six wedges and serve at once.

TASTY TOPPINGS
FOR PLANT-BASED BURGERS

Whether you buy one of the many excellent plant-based burgers available these days or make your own (page 228), go the extra step of piling on the toppings! It's not much work, and those few extra layers of veggies and other flavors make a simple meal option even more satisfying.

Try the combinations listed here, and vary the type of bread you use—kaiser rolls and English muffins work as well as burger buns, and you can also stuff burgers into pita bread. Add vegan mayo and sriracha to your list of standard condiments along with mustard and ketchup.

Crisp-cooked plant-based bacon, vegan cheese slices, tomato, and wilted spinach

Caramelized onions and bell peppers, barbecue sauce, and thinly sliced dill pickles

Any kind of simple slaw, vegan cheese slices, and bread-and-butter pickle slices

Thousand Island-ish Dressing (page 129), sliced tomatoes, and green sprouts

Hummus, sauerkraut, sliced avocado, and sliced red onion

Guacamole, arugula or shredded lettuce, and pico de gallo or salsa

Wilted mushrooms, vegan cheese slices, sliced tomatoes, and tahini dressing

Vegan pesto, roasted red peppers, and vegan mozzarella slices

CLASSIC SANDWICHES

YOU CAN MAKE WITHOUT A RECIPE

Sandwich fans who are giving up meat, or easing away from it, should be glad to know that not only won't they have to give up their favorite sandwiches; they also won't need to follow exact recipes for them. Here are a few suggestions—most of which involve plant-based bacon or Smokey Tempeh Strips (page 224):

CLASSIC CLUB SANDWICH: Club sandwiches are double-deckers, one layer of which is basically a BLT. Start with whatever plant-based bacon you prefer. Crisp it up in a small skillet, then layer it with lettuce, tomato, and vegan mayo. The second layer consists of a few deli slices and a slice of cheese, so just swap plant-based versions for the originals. Spread the bread with mustard. The most challenging part of these stacked sandwiches is holding them together; a cocktail toothpick can assist with that.

VEGAN ELVIS: The original weird but good—really good—sandwich is named for Elvis Presley, the pop icon of the 1950s and '60s. Supposedly this was his favorite sandwich. Spread peanut butter and jam on whole-grain bread. Top with a layer of sliced bananas and crisped bacon (in this case, your favorite plant-based variety). It makes a hearty breakfast sandwich and is good for a portable lunch.

BLT SANDWICH OR WRAP: Oh, so easy—and obvious! Simply cook your favorite kind of plant-based bacon and layer it on whole-grain toast or in wraps with lettuce, tomato, and vegan mayo. If you want to add a little something extra, sliced avocado is most welcome.

ITALIAN MEATBALL OR CHICK'N PARMESAN SUB: Warm up 4 plant-based meatballs or enough breaded chick'n nuggets to fill a hero roll. Split the roll lengthwise and slather some marinara sauce on both sides. Arrange the meatballs or nuggets on the bottom of the roll, then sprinkle with vegan mozzarella-style shreds.

It's best to warm these in a not-too-hot oven just long enough to melt the cheese. If you're only making one sandwich, a toaster oven is fine. Microwaving the finished heroes until the cheese melts works, too, but don't overdo it—30 to 40 seconds should be enough; otherwise the roll can get mushy.

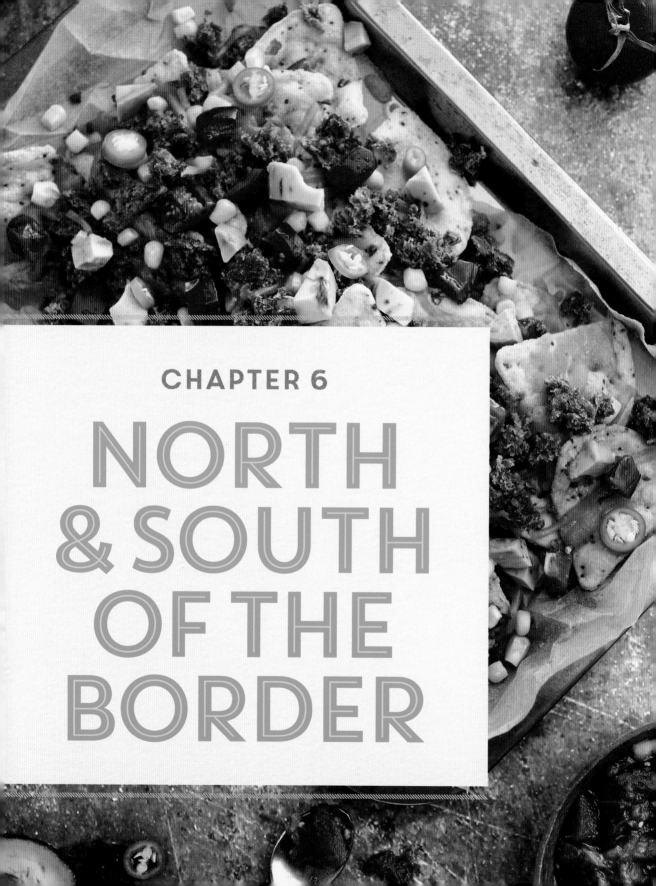

CHAPTER 6

NORTH & SOUTH OF THE BORDER

DURING RECENT YEARS IT has become so
much easier to make homemade versions of the specialties variously
characterized as Mexican, southwestern, and Tex-Mex. When I was
working on one of my early cookbooks eons ago, I had trouble finding
corn tortillas that didn't taste like cardboard and flour tortillas that didn't
contain lard. Cilantro? Who had ever heard of that? Other ingredients
we take for granted now, such as fresh chili peppers, had to be searched
for in ethnic groceries, which was actually fun but often out of the way.

Now most any supermarket offers fresh tortillas of various kinds,
great ready-made salsas for the busy or lazy among us, and cuisine-
specific seasonings. And I'm not just talking about supermarkets in
North America. While on vacation in Reykjavik, Iceland, I came across a
big colorful display of make-your-own soft taco ingredients, including
fresh tortillas, mango salsa, and a dry seasoning mix for the protein of
one's choice. "Ready in 10 minutes!" the sign proclaimed.

And that's part of the beauty of this type of cuisine. Cooking time
is minimal, and most everything can be assembled at the last minute—
even at the table. And these days, added to the roster of easy-to-find
ingredients for tacos, burritos, and the like are the plant-based proteins
that not long ago didn't exist. Plant-based chorizo, beefy ground, even
fishless fillets—they're all ready and waiting to fill your tortillas.

BARBECUE
BEEFY TACOS

MAKES 8 TO 10 TACOS

WITH SO MANY PLANT protein choices now available, it has become ridiculously easy to make vegan tacos. You can make your own beefy crumbles with a few simple ingredients or use one of the many prepared products on the market. One of my favorites is unadorned pea-protein crumbles, which offer a blank canvas for your own flavorings and seasonings.

Feel free to use other kinds of protein crumbles or vegan chorizo, in which case you can cut back on the amount of homemade barbecue sauce given here. You even have the option of using crumbled vegan burgers, which, depending on the brand, can be a whole-food route to vegan crumbles (if they're made from black beans, for example). These tacos have plenty of eye appeal, and the contrast between the barbecue-flavored protein and cool slaw is fantastic. Let guests assemble their own tacos at the table—it's easier and more fun.

PLANT PROTEIN OPTIONS

Plant-based crumbles or chorizo

4 beef-style vegan burgers, crumbled

1 recipe Tempeh and Walnut Ground (page 214; if you use this option, omit the barbecue sauce and proceed directly to sautéing)

10 to 12 ounces dry pea-protein crumbles, rehydrated, or other plant protein crumbles (see options at left)

½ to 1 cup bottled barbecue sauce or Quick No-Cook Barbecue Sauce (page 240)

4 cups shredded cabbage (see note)

½ cup vegan mayonnaise

8 to 10 soft taco-size (6- to 8-inch) flour or corn tortillas

1 medium ripe avocado, peeled, pitted, and finely diced

Coarsely chopped fresh cilantro leaves to taste

Lime wedges for serving (optional)

1 Heat a medium skillet and add the rehydrated or prepared crumbles. Depending on what you're using, you'll need between ½ cup and 1 cup barbecue sauce. If using pea-protein crumbles, you'll want to use the full cup of sauce, since they need to absorb lots of flavor. If using any of the commercially prepared crumbles or crumbled vegan burgers, start with ½ cup sauce and taste, then add more if desired.

2 In a large skillet, cook the protein of your choice with the barbecue sauce over medium-high heat for 8 to 10 minutes, or until the protein begins to brown lightly, stirring often.

3 Meanwhile, combine the cabbage with the vegan mayonnaise in a bowl and stir.

4 To assemble the tacos, spread the tortillas with the cabbage mixture, followed by the protein. Top each with avocado and cilantro. Serve with lime wedges if desired to add a final burst of flavor. Serve at once and eat out of hand.

NOTE: *Mix in a little red cabbage if you like, or use packaged preshredded cabbage.*

PULLED-PROTEIN
TACOS / WITH FRUITY CORN-PINEAPPLE SALSA

MAKES 6 TO 8 TACOS

THIS TACO RECIPE IS always a hit, each time I make it. Is it the citrus-spiked pulled protein, or the subtly sweet corn-pineapple salsa? Most likely it's the way those two components complement and contrast with each other. These tacos might look and taste festive, but they're easy enough to enjoy as a weeknight meal.

FOR THE FRUITY CORN-PINEAPPLE SALSA

¾ cup cooked fresh or thawed frozen corn kernels

½ cup finely chopped fresh or well-drained canned pineapple or mango

Juice of 1 lime

½ cup finely chopped red onion

½ medium red bell pepper, finely chopped

Fresh cilantro leaves to taste

1 jalapeño pepper, seeded and minced

FOR THE TACOS

1 tablespoon extra-virgin olive oil

½ cup finely chopped red onion

½ medium red bell pepper, chopped

8 to 10 ounces plant-based pulled protein (chop more finely if chunky)

Juice of 1 orange

2 teaspoons chili powder

6 to 8 soft taco-size (6- to 8-inch) flour or corn tortillas

GARNISHES (OPTIONAL)

Lime wedges

Hot sauce

1 Combine the salsa ingredients in a small bowl. Stir and set aside.

2 Heat the oil in a medium skillet. Add the onion and sauté over medium heat until translucent. Add the bell pepper and continue to sauté until the onion is golden.

3 Add the protein, orange juice, and chili powder. Increase the heat to medium-high and continue to cook until the juice reduces and nicely glazes the protein, 5 to 7 minutes.

4 To assemble, distribute the protein mixture among the tortillas. Spoon a little of the salsa over the protein, then fold over. Eat at once. Pass lime wedges and hot sauce, if desired, at the table.

FISHLIKE
TACOS / WITH AVOCADO-CILANTRO CREAM

MAKES 6 TO 8 TACOS

FISH TACOS BECAME A thing long after I gave up seafood, so I never got to puzzle out what the appeal might be. But as we all know, they're hugely popular, so there must be something about them. I have a theory that this preparation is as much about the embellishments as it is about the fish—or in our case, plant-based fish fillets, a recent innovation in the plant-protein world.

FOR THE CREAMY SLAW

4 cups thinly sliced green cabbage or bagged coleslaw

¼ cup chopped fresh cilantro

2 scallions, thinly sliced

½ cup vegan sour cream or vegan mayonnaise, or ¼ cup vegan sour cream and ¼ cup vegan mayonnaise

Juice of ½ lime

FOR THE AVOCADO CREAM

1 medium ripe avocado, pitted, peeled, and mashed

¼ cup vegan sour cream

¼ cup finely chopped fresh cilantro

Juice of ½ lime

FOR THE TACOS

1 (8- to 10-ounce) package breaded plant-based fish fillets

6 to 8 soft taco-size (6- to 8-inch) flour or corn tortillas

TOPPINGS (OPTIONAL)

Picante sauce to taste

Sriracha to taste

1 jalapeño pepper, seeded and thinly sliced

1 Combine the creamy slaw ingredients in a mixing bowl and stir.

2 In a shallow bowl, combine the avocado cream ingredients and stir. If you want this to be extra smooth, combine the ingredients in a food processor and process until smooth.

3 Cut the plant-based fish fillets into narrow strips, then heat according to package directions.

4 To assemble the tacos, lay the tortillas on a clean work surface or serving platter. In the center third of each tortilla, spread some slaw (you may have some left over, but that's fine—don't overload), followed by some plant-based fish and a dollop of avocado cream. Finish with a drizzle of picante sauce or sriracha and a few slices of jalapeño if desired. Eat out of hand at once.

LIME-MARINATED
CHICK'N FAJITAS / OR TACOS

MAKES 8 TACOS

WHAT'S BEST ABOUT SERVING fajitas and tacos is that everyone at the table participates in creating the meal, and no one seems to mind. Filled with lime-marinated protein, these are delectable and so easy to prepare.

The protein filling, embellished with lots of bell pepper, can be served loosely rolled up for fajitas or folded in half for tacos. They have the same great flavor either way. Serve with fresh corn in the summer, and in the fall and winter, russet or sweet potato oven fries are a perfect side dish.

PLANT PROTEIN OPTIONS

Plant-based chick'n

½ recipe Chicken-Style Seitan Cutlets (page 222)

Tempeh

Baked tofu

8 (6- to 8-inch) soft flour or corn tortillas

3 tablespoons freshly squeezed lime juice

1½ tablespoons extra-virgin olive oil

2 teaspoons chili powder

1 teaspoon ground cumin

½ teaspoon dried oregano

8 to 10 ounces chicken-style plant protein (see options at left), cut into small pieces or shredded

1 medium green bell pepper, cut into narrow strips

1 medium red bell pepper, cut into narrow strips

FOR SERVING

Shredded lettuce (romaine works well)

Prepared salsa

Fresh cilantro sprigs

Vegan sour cream

Picante sauce

1 If you want to warm the tortillas, preheat the oven to 300°F. Wrap the tortillas in foil and place them in the oven for 5 minutes or so. If the tortillas are fresh and pliable, you can skip this step, but at least bring them to room temperature.

2 Set out the items for serving before starting, because the rest of the preparation goes quickly. Place the lettuce, salsa, cilantro, and sour cream in separate serving bowls and set them on the table. Place a bottle of picante sauce on the table for those who like hot stuff.

3 Combine the lime juice, oil, chili powder, cumin, and oregano in a medium mixing bowl and whisk. Add the plant-based chicken and toss gently. Add the bell pepper strips and toss again.

4 Heat a large skillet over medium heat, then add the plant-protein mixture, liquid and all. Increase the heat to high and cook, stirring frequently, for 5 to 7 minutes, or until sizzling hot and touched with brown spots. Remove from the heat and cover.

5 Place one or two tortillas on each serving plate. Have guests place a few strips of the protein mixture in the center of their tortillas and garnish with lettuce, salsa, cilantro, sour cream, and picante sauce as desired. Roll up the tortillas or fold in half and eat out of hand.

CARNE ASADA
FRIES

CARNE ASADA FRIES STARTED as a food trend in San Diego in the 1990s, and from there they became popular nationwide. A combination of french fries, avocado, sour cream, and, in its original form, grilled strip steak (the very definition of carne asada), this dish is not uncommon on Mexican restaurant menus, even in vegan form. In fact, that's how I discovered it. The concept seems odd, but the preparation is really good.

This dish is usually made with russet potatoes, and you can use them if you prefer. But sweet potatoes add another lovely layer of flavor, not to mention color. Let's keep it super easy by using organic frozen sweet potato fries.

FOR THE CARNE ASADA AND FRIES

1 tablespoon extra-virgin olive oil

2 tablespoons freshly squeezed lime juice

2 tablespoons orange juice

¼ cup prepared salsa

1 teaspoon chili powder

½ teaspoon ground cumin

8 to 10 ounces steak-style plant protein, cut into strips

1 (20-ounce) package frozen organic sweet potato fries

TOPPINGS

2 medium ripe avocados, pitted, peeled, and mashed

Juice of ½ lime

½ cup halved fresh cherry tomatoes or diced ripe fresh tomato

Fresh cilantro leaves

Vegan sour cream

1 jalapeño pepper, seeded and sliced

Prepared salsa

Lime wedges

1 Preheat the oven to 425°F. Line a baking sheet or roasting pan with parchment paper.

2 Combine the oil, lime and orange juices, salsa, chili powder, and cumin in a shallow container and whisk. Add the plant protein, stir, and allow to marinate for at least 30 minutes.

3 Arrange the sweet potato fries in a single layer on the prepared baking sheet or roasting pan. Bake for 20 to 25 minutes (or according to package directions).

4 Combine the mashed avocados with the lime juice in a small bowl and stir.

Recipe continues

5 About 10 minutes before the fries are done, heat a medium skillet over medium-high heat. Add the beefy strips and marinade and cook until nicely glazed and sizzling hot.

6 To assemble, transfer the baked fries to a serving platter. Scatter the beefy strips over them, followed by the tomato and cilantro. Traditionally, a dollop of the mashed avocado and a dollop of sour cream are placed next to each other on one side of the platter, but you can put those in separate small bowls if you prefer.

7 Place the jalapeño slices, salsa, and lime wedges in separate small bowls.

8 Have everyone serve themselves from the serving platter, and pass around the toppings at the table.

CARNE ASADA
TACOS

MAKES 4 TACOS

CARNE ASADA IS A dish consisting of steak strips marinated in citrus juices and grilled or otherwise cooked over high heat. This version replaces the beef with steak-style plant protein, which can be cut into strips and used as taco filling. It's equally good made with seitan—I've made it with both, to great success. This is a satisfying alternative to the more common ground-filled vegan tacos and just as easy to make.

FOR THE CARNE ASADA

1 tablespoon extra-virgin olive oil

2 tablespoons freshly squeezed lime juice

2 tablespoons orange juice

1 teaspoon chili powder

½ teaspoon ground cumin

8 to 10 ounces steak-style plant protein, cut into strips

FOR ASSEMBLY

4 soft taco-size (6- to 8-inch) flour or corn tortillas

Finely shredded lettuce or cabbage to taste

Prepared pico de gallo or salsa to taste

1 medium ripe avocado, pitted, peeled, and mashed with a little lime juice, or prepared guacamole to taste

GARNISHES (OPTIONAL)

Lime wedges

Fresh cilantro leaves

Jalapeño pepper slices

1 Combine the oil, lime and orange juices, chili powder, and cumin in a shallow container and whisk. Add the beefy strips, stir, and allow to marinate for at least 30 minutes.

2 When you're ready to cook, heat a lightly oiled grill pan or skillet over medium-high heat. Arrange the protein strips on the surface and drizzle with the remaining marinade. Turn the strips after a few minutes.

3 Cook until sizzling hot and turning crisp on most sides.

4 To assemble, arrange a little lettuce in the center of each tortilla. Top with the beefy strips, followed by pico de gallo and some mashed avocado. Embellish with any or all of the garnishes and serve at once.

MEATY VEGGIE BURRITOS

MAKES 8 BURRITOS

SOME MEXICAN AND TEX-MEX eateries offer vegetable burritos as a meatless option, with refried beans either within the burrito or on the side. I like them within, because they help hold everything together. In this recipe, that's especially true, since we're making the burritos extra substantial with plant protein. These yummy burritos can accommodate many kinds of plant protein, from chicken-style strips to spicy chorizo, for a different flavor profile each time you make them. You can also vary the vegetables suggested here, depending on what you have on hand.

PLANT PROTEIN OPTIONS

Plant-based chorizo or ground

Plant-based chick'n

Beef-style plant protein

1 recipe Tempeh and Mushroom Chorizo (page 215)

1 tablespoon extra-virgin olive oil

1 medium onion, quartered and thinly sliced

8 to 10 ounces plant protein (see options at left), finely chopped

1 medium red bell pepper, cut into short, narrow strips

1 cup diced zucchini or yellow summer squash

½ cup cleaned, stemmed, and sliced cremini (baby bella) mushrooms

2 big handfuls baby spinach, arugula, or power greens (see page 56)

¼ cup fresh cilantro leaves, or more to taste

1 (15-ounce) can vegan refried beans

8 burrito-size (10-inch) flour tortillas, at room temperature or gently warmed

Prepared salsa to taste

1 cup vegan Cheddar- or pepper Jack–style cheese shreds

1 Heat the oil in a large skillet. Add the onion and sauté over medium heat until translucent. Add the plant protein and bell pepper and continue to sauté until everything in the skillet is golden, about 8 minutes.

2 Add the squash and mushrooms. Continue to sauté until they soften, about 2 minutes.

3 Add the spinach and cover; cook just until wilted. Add the cilantro, stir, and remove from the heat.

4 If the refried beans are too thick to spread, combine them in a mixing bowl with a little water to loosen the consistency.

5 To assemble the burritos, spread the refried beans over most of the surface of each tortilla.

6 Divide the vegetable mixture among the tortillas, placing it more or less in the center. Add a generous dollop of salsa and a sprinkling of cheese to each. Fold two ends over the vegetable mixture, then roll up and place one or two burritos seam side down on each serving plate.

7 Cut in half crosswise and serve at once.

BIG CHORIZO
QUESADILLAS / WITH GREENS & REFRIED BEANS

**MAKES 4 LARGE
QUESADILLAS**

THESE KNIFE-AND-FORK QUESADILLAS ARE packed with plant-based chorizo, refried beans, fresh vegetables, and fruity salsa—a veritable feast wrapped in the largest possible tortillas. Each quesadilla is a generous meal in itself; cut in half, it's still quite hefty if you're serving a filling grain or potato side dish alongside.

1 (5-ounce) package baby spinach or power greens (see page 56)

1 (15-ounce) can vegan refried beans

4 (12-inch) soft flour tortillas or wraps

Picante sauce or other hot seasoning to taste

4 to 5 ounces plant-based chorizo or ½ recipe Tempeh and Mushroom Chorizo (page 215)

2 large or 3 medium firm ripe fresh tomatoes, halved and sliced

1½ cups Cheddar- or pepper Jack–style vegan cheese shreds

Prepared pineapple or mango salsa to taste

1 medium ripe avocado, pitted, peeled, and sliced

1 Preheat the oven to 400°F.

2 Rinse the greens and steam them in a wide skillet or stir-fry pan for a minute or so, just until barely wilted. Transfer to a colander and press out the liquid.

3 If the refried beans are too thick to spread, combine them in a mixing bowl with a little water to loosen the consistency.

4 Lay a tortilla on a baking sheet. Spread half of it with one-fourth of each of the following, in this order: the refried beans, picante sauce, chorizo, greens, tomato slices, and cheese. Fold over to cover. Repeat with the remaining tortillas. Use an additional baking sheet if necessary.

5 Bake for 10 minutes, or until the tortillas begin to turn golden and crisp.

6 To serve, place one whole or one half quesadilla on each serving plate. Top with salsa and avocado slices and serve, passing extra salsa and picante sauce at the table. These are definitely knife-and-fork quesadillas— they're too hefty to eat out of hand!

EASIEST EVER
ENCHILADA BAKE

SERVES 6 TO 8

WHAT'S EASIER THAN ROLLING and filling a dozen or so enchiladas? Layering the ingredients in one big casserole dish. And what's even easier than that? Doing away with the layering, which, though not difficult, still requires dividing all the tasty ingredients just so.

This hearty casserole works well with either a chickeny or beefy spin. A quick turn in the oven leaves you just enough time to make a colorful salad or slaw.

PLANT PROTEIN OPTIONS

Plant-based beef-style ground or crumbles

Plant-based chorizo

4 beef-style vegan burgers, crumbled

1 recipe Tempeh and Mushroom Chorizo (page 215)

1 tablespoon extra-virgin olive oil

1 medium red onion, finely chopped, divided

8 to 10 ounces plant-based beef-style crumbles or ground (see options at left)

1 (15-ounce) can pink, red, or pinto beans, drained and rinsed

1 (14-ounce) can crushed tomatoes

1 (1.5-ounce) packet taco seasoning

2 cups thawed frozen corn kernels

10 to 12 (6-inch) soft corn tortillas, cut into 1-inch pieces

1 cup prepared salsa, divided

1½ cups vegan Cheddar- or pepper Jack–style cheese shreds, divided

¼ cup chopped fresh cilantro

1 jalapeño pepper, seeded and sliced (optional)

1 Preheat the oven to 400°F.

2 Heat the oil in a large skillet or stir-fry pan. Measure ¼ cup chopped onion and set it aside for the topping. Sauté the remaining onion over medium heat until golden, about 8 minutes.

3 Add the crumbles and sauté for 5 to 8 minutes, stirring often, until lightly browned.

4 Add the beans, crushed tomatoes, and taco seasoning. Stir, then add the corn, tortillas, half the salsa, and 1 cup of the cheese.

5 Remove from the heat and transfer the mixture to a lightly oiled 2-quart casserole dish. Spread the remaining salsa and cheese over the top.

6 Bake for 20 minutes, or until the cheese is nicely melted. Remove from the oven and top with the cilantro, jalapeño (if desired), and reserved red onion.

7 Let stand for a few minutes, then cut into wedges or squares to serve.

TEX-MEX
RICE BOWLS

SERVES 4

I USUALLY SHY AWAY from recipes with long (or even longish) ingredients lists—and that goes double for dishes that require more than one cooking pot. But I promise you that this recipe is super easy to make and so festive to serve.

While the rice cooks, you can prepare everything else, and if you use white rice you'll be eating within half an hour (brown rice will take an additional fifteen minutes or so). The nice thing about this recipe is that your plant-based protein is combined with nourishing, inexpensive black beans. And between you and me, if on occasion you prefer to make this only with beans, it's just as good.

PLANT PROTEIN OPTIONS

Plant-based ground or crumbles

Plant-based chorizo

2 beef-style vegan burgers, crumbled

1 recipe Tempeh and Mushroom Chorizo (page 215)

FOR THE RICE

1 tablespoon extra-virgin olive oil

1 medium onion, finely chopped

2 cloves garlic, minced

½ bell pepper, any color, finely chopped

1 cup uncooked long-grain white or brown rice

1 cup prepared salsa

2 teaspoons chili powder

2 to 2½ cups water, plus more if desired

FOR THE PROTEIN

1 tablespoon extra-virgin olive oil

4 to 5 ounces plant-based beef-style ground or crumbles (see options at left)

1 cup cooked or canned black beans, drained and rinsed

½ cup prepared salsa, or more to taste

1 teaspoon chili powder

FOR SERVING

1 medium ripe avocado, pitted, peeled, and well mashed with a little lemon or lime juice, or prepared guacamole to taste

1 cup vegan Cheddar- or pepper Jack–style cheese shreds

1 medium ripe fresh tomato, finely diced

Shredded lettuce to taste

Vegan sour cream to taste (optional)

Prepared salsa or picante sauce to taste

Recipe continues

1 To make the rice, heat the oil in a large skillet or stir-fry pan. Add the onion and sauté over medium-low heat until translucent.

2 Add the garlic and bell pepper and continue to sauté until the vegetables are golden, about 5 minutes

3 Add the rice, salsa, chili powder, and water (use 2 cups for white rice, 2½ cups for brown). Bring to a slow boil, then lower the heat, cover, and simmer gently until the water is absorbed, 15 to 20 minutes for the white rice and 30 to 35 minutes for the brown. If you prefer a more tender grain, add ½ cup additional water and cook until absorbed.

4 Meanwhile, to make the protein, heat the oil in a small skillet. Add the ground and sauté over medium-high heat for 2 to 3 minutes. Add the beans, salsa, and chili powder and continue to cook for 5 minutes or so, until sizzling hot. Set aside.

5 To assemble, divide the rice among four wide, shallow bowls. Mound about ½ cup of the protein mixture on the rice, either in the center or off to the side. (You'll likely have more than you need for this arrangement, so you can keep the protein mixture handy for anyone who wants seconds.) Spoon the avocado mixture (or guacamole) and vegan cheese over the rice in each bowl.

6 Fill in the remaining space with tomatoes and shredded lettuce. Add a dollop of sour cream if desired. Serve at once, passing salsa or picante sauce at the table.

BEEFY NACHOS GRANDES

SERVES 4 AS A MEAL, 8 AS A SNACK

VEGAN NACHOS CAN BE fantastic party fare or even an emergency dinner. They're also a great way to persuade your skeptical friends to take a walk on the veg side. Though the ingredient amounts in this recipe are enough to make a hefty platter of nachos, you can also scale the recipe down to make a single serving on a regular-size plate. Just layer on a bit less—no need for exact measuring. And if you don't want to run the oven, simply arrange the nachos on a microwaveable platter and "nuke" them until the cheese is melted—it usually takes less than a minute.

PLANT PROTEIN OPTIONS

Plant-based ground or crumbles

Plant-based chorizo

2 beef-style vegan burgers, crumbled

1 recipe Tempeh and Mushroom Chorizo (page 215)

1 tablespoon extra-virgin olive oil

4 to 5 ounces plant-based beef-style crumbles or ground (see options at left)

Good-quality tortilla chips (about half of a 13-ounce bag), as needed

1 cup thawed frozen corn kernels

1 (8-ounce) package vegan Cheddar- or pepper Jack–style cheese shreds

1 or 2 jalapeño peppers, sliced (optional)

1 medium ripe avocado, pitted, peeled, and diced

2 medium ripe fresh tomatoes, diced, or 1 cup fresh cherry or grape tomatoes, halved

1 (8-ounce) jar prepared salsa

1 Preheat the oven to 400°F.

2 Heat the oil in a medium skillet. Add the crumbles and sauté over medium heat until lightly browned, about 8 minutes.

3 Spread the tortilla chips on a large baking sheet or ovenproof platter. Sprinkle with the corn, crumbles, cheese shreds, and sliced jalapeños, if desired.

4 Bake for 8 minutes, or until the cheese is nicely melted.

5 Top the nachos with the avocado and tomatoes. Pass the salsa at the table.

6 Have guests scoop some of the nachos onto individual plates if you're serving them as a meal or just dig in with their hands if you're serving them as a snack or an appetizer.

Beefy Nachos Grandes,
page 167

CHAPTER 7

COOL & HOT SALADS

I ASSOCIATE SALADS (one of my favorite things to make and eat) with vegetables, unsurprisingly. So at first, it didn't even occur to me to include a salads chapter in this book. But then, this is America, the land where meat has found its way into practically every type of dish. When I remembered this fact, I was overjoyed to discover an array of classic meaty salads that I could convert to plant-based versions.

Chicken-based and tuna-based salads are an intrinsic part of the culinary landscape. Bacon gets tossed into many a salad, and, going outside of Western traditions, I found a couple of beefy Asian-inspired salads that were perfect for a plant-protein makeover.

During the process of creating the recipes for this book, I was delighted that the salads I served to family and friends were as successful as the comfort foods. A couple of standouts were the Teriyaki Chick'n Salad and the Thai-Inspired Beefy Salad. Perhaps these, along with some of the other salads presented in this chapter, will become your favorites as well.

CURRIED
CHICK'N SALAD
WITH GRAPES & ALMONDS

SERVES 4 TO 6

HERE'S A CLASSIC SALAD that proves how easy and delicious it is to amp up an already plant-strong dish. As it is in the original, the protein here is embellished with grapes, celery, and scallions and enveloped in a curry-flavored vegan mayo. Spread this easy and refreshing salad on fresh bread or dollop it onto lettuce leaves.

PLANT PROTEIN OPTIONS

Plant-based chick'n

½ recipe Chicken-Style Seitan Cutlets (page 222)

Baked tofu

FOR THE DRESSING
½ cup vegan mayonnaise

1 teaspoon prepared yellow mustard

1 teaspoon curry powder

1 teaspoon sweet pickle relish (optional)

FOR THE CHICK'N
8 ounces chicken-style plant protein (see options at left), chopped or diced

1 cup halved red seedless grapes

2 to 3 celery stalks, diced

2 scallions, thinly sliced

Freshly ground pepper to taste

FOR SERVING
Tender lettuce leaves (such as butter or Boston), mixed baby greens, or fresh bread slices (optional)

Toasted sliced almonds, chopped walnuts, or sunflower seeds (optional)

1 Combine the dressing ingredients in a small bowl and set aside.

2 In a small mixing bowl, combine the protein, grapes, celery, and scallions. Add the dressing and stir. Season with pepper.

3 Serve as a straight-up salad by lining a small serving platter or individual plates with salad greens and mounding the chick'n salad over them. If your lettuce has cuplike leaves (as Boston lettuce does, for example), you can dollop it into them. Fancy!

4 Alternatively, serve as an open-faced sandwich by placing some lettuce on a slice of bread and topping it with a scoop of the chick'n salad.

5 Sprinkle with nuts or seeds, if desired, and enjoy.

BUFFALO
CHICK'N SALAD

SERVES 4 TO 6

THE BUFFALO TREATMENT HAS gotten to be a familiar formula—chicken wings cooked in a combination of butter and Frank's hot sauce, served alongside raw carrots and celery with a creamy dressing, usually blue cheese or ranch. In the plant-based world, the wings are made from some sort of plant protein, tofu, or cauliflower.

For this recipe, all the lively textures and flavors of the Buffalo composition are turned into an easy salad. Vegan ranch dressing isn't always easy to find, so I supply an easy recipe.

PLANT PROTEIN OPTIONS

Plant-based chick'n (any style, including breaded nuggets or wings)

½ recipe Chicken-Style Seitan Cutlets (page 222)

1 medium head romaine or other dark green lettuce, thinly sliced

1 cup grated carrots

2 large or 3 medium celery stalks, thinly sliced

1 scallion, thinly sliced

Bottled vegan ranch dressing or homemade Vegan Ranch Dressing (page 238) to taste

2 tablespoons vegan butter

1 tablespoon Frank's or other hot sauce, or to taste

8 to 11 ounces plant-based chicken (see options at left), cut into thin slices or bite-size pieces

1 Combine the lettuce, carrots, celery, and scallion in a large, shallow serving bowl and toss. Add enough dressing to coat generously and toss again.

2 Heat the butter and hot sauce together in a medium skillet. Add the chick'n and sauté over medium-high heat, stirring often, until golden and crisp on most sides, about 8 minutes.

3 Arrange the chick'n over the vegetables and serve immediately, passing the remaining dressing at the table.

RICE NOODLE
"STEAK" SALAD

SERVES 4   **RICE NOODLES JOIN FORCES** with strips of beefy plant protein, cucumbers, and cilantro in a Thai-inspired cold dish that's both hearty and refreshing. Do try the mint—it adds such a nice flavor.

FOR THE DRESSING

¼ to ½ cup coarsely chopped fresh cilantro leaves

Juice of 1 lime, or more to taste

⅓ cup bottled sweet chili sauce

2 to 3 teaspoons grated fresh or squeeze-bottle ginger

FOR THE SALAD

1 medium cucumber, halved lengthwise and thinly sliced

¼ cup rice vinegar or apple cider vinegar

1 tablespoon natural granulated sugar

1 (4- to 6-ounce) bundle fine or wide rice noodles

6 to 8 radishes, thinly sliced

2 to 3 scallions, thinly sliced

½ cup fresh cilantro leaves

Fresh mint leaves to taste (optional)

1 tablespoon neutral vegetable oil (such as safflower) or dark sesame oil

8 to 10 ounces steak-style plant protein, cut into thin strips

Salt and freshly ground pepper to taste

Sesame seeds or chopped peanuts for garnish (optional)

1 Combine the dressing ingredients in a small bowl. Stir and set aside.

2 Combine the cucumber, vinegar, and sugar in a small bowl. Toss and set aside.

3 Cook the rice noodles according to package directions. When done, drain and rinse under cold running water until fairly cool. These noodles are very long, so reach into the colander and cut here and there with kitchen shears to shorten. Drain well again, then transfer to a serving bowl.

4 Add the radishes, scallions, and cilantro to the bowl along with the cucumbers—liquid and all. Add the chili-lime dressing. Toss thoroughly.

5 Heat the oil in a medium skillet. Add the plant protein and sauté over medium-high heat, stirring often, until golden and crisp on most sides. Stir into the noodle mixture while still hot. Season with salt and pepper and serve. Garnish individual servings with sesame seeds or chopped peanuts if desired.

THAI-INSPIRED
BEEFY SALAD

SERVES 4 TO 6

WHILE USING MY FAMILY and friends as guinea pigs for some of this book's recipes, I discovered this salad was a standout. When you try it, I hope you'll agree. Steak-style plant protein has become readily available, and the key to its success in this salad is to let it get nice and crisp in the pan. A lime-flavored dressing pulls all the ingredients together.

FOR THE DRESSING

Juice of 1 lime

¼ cup bottled teriyaki or Korean barbecue sauce, or homemade Teriyaki Sauce (page 241)

2 teaspoons natural granulated sugar

1 teaspoon sriracha or other hot sauce, or more to taste

1 tablespoon sesame oil

FOR THE PROTEIN

Safflower or other neutral vegetable oil for the pan

8 to 10 ounces steak-style plant protein, cut into thin strips

FOR THE SALAD

Mixed baby greens or shredded lettuce to taste

2 medium fresh ripe tomatoes, diced

½ medium cucumber, halved lengthwise and sliced

½ red onion, sliced into half-moons

¼ cup fresh cilantro leaves

GARNISHES

Jalapeño pepper slices (optional)

Lime slices (optional)

1 Combine the dressing ingredients in a small bowl and stir.

2 To make the protein, heat just enough oil to coat the bottom of a medium skillet. Add the steak-style strips and sauté over medium-high heat until golden and starting to turn crisp on most sides, about 6 minutes.

3 Pour in about 2 tablespoons of the dressing and continue to sauté until the strips are nicely glazed, just a minute or two longer. Remove from the heat and cover.

4 To assemble the salad, line a large platter with the greens, then scatter the tomatoes, cucumber, onion, and cilantro over them.

5 Drizzle the vegetables evenly with the remaining dressing, then top with the steak-style strips.

6 Garnish with a few jalapeño and lime slices if desired. Either serve at once, while the plant protein is still warm, or let cool to room temperature.

LAYERED
TACO SALAD

SERVES 4

I HAVE A THING for salads that are both hot and cool, and this black bean taco salad is one of my favorites. It's a fast and fun main dish that has it all—salad veggies, high-protein beans, and two "yum factor" ingredients: good-quality tortilla chips and vegan cheese.

For a light summer meal, corn on the cob is a nice addition. For a hearty cold-weather meal, pair this with a big batch of roasted vegetables or baked sweet potatoes.

PLANT PROTEIN OPTIONS

Plant-based ground or crumbles

2 beef-style vegan burgers, crumbled

1 recipe Tempeh and Mushroom Chorizo (page 215)

4 to 6 ounces plant-based ground or crumbles (see options at left)

1 (15-ounce) can red, black, or pinto beans, drained and rinsed

1 cup prepared salsa

2 teaspoons barbecue seasoning, or more to taste

4 cups mixed greens or shredded lettuce, or to taste

Freshly squeezed lime juice to taste

2 small fresh ripe tomatoes, diced

1 medium ripe avocado, pitted, peeled, and diced

Good-quality tortilla chips to taste

1 cup vegan Cheddar- or pepper Jack–style cheese shreds

GARNISHES
Chopped fresh cilantro (optional)

Sliced jalapeño peppers (optional)

1 Combine the ground, beans, salsa, and barbecue seasoning in a skillet. Sauté over medium heat until sizzling hot, stirring occasionally, about 8 minutes.

2 Line four medium serving plates or bowls with the greens and drizzle a little lime juice over them.

3 Combine the tomatoes and avocado in a small bowl and toss with a little lime juice as well.

4 Layer some tortilla chips over the greens on each plate in more or less a single layer. Follow with one-fourth of the hot protein mixture, one-fourth of the cheese shreds, and one-fourth of the tomato-avocado mixture on each plate. Alternatively, layer the ingredients on a single serving platter and let guests serve themselves.

5 Garnish with cilantro and/or jalapeños if desired and eat at once, while the beefy bean mixture is hot and the chips are crisp.

TERIYAKI
CHICK'N SALAD

SERVES 4

WHO WOULD HAVE THOUGHT that a chick'n salad could offer such a dazzling rainbow of colors and textures? That's exactly what you get with this composed platter, which is a contemporary innovation rather than a classic. I find that that scallopine-style or cutlet-style plant-based chicken works best for this, but use what you have on hand or is readily available. It will all taste (and look) fantastic.

PLANT PROTEIN OPTIONS

Plant-based chick'n, preferably scallopine-style or cutlet-style

½ recipe Chicken-Style Seitan Cutlets (page 222)

Baked tofu

¼ cup bottled teriyaki sauce or homemade Teriyaki Sauce (page 241)

8 to 10 ounces plant-based chicken (see options at left), cut into narrow strips

Mixed baby greens or shredded lettuce to taste

2 large celery stalks, thinly sliced

1 heaping cup fresh or drained canned pineapple chunks and/or sections of small orange, such as mandarin or clementine

½ medium bell pepper, any color, cut into strips

1 cup halved fresh cherry or grape tomatoes

½ cup whole or halved cashews

Bottled sesame-ginger dressing to taste

1 Heat the teriyaki sauce in a medium skillet. Add the chick'n and cook over medium-high heat on both sides, stirring often, until nicely glazed, about 5 minutes. Remove from the heat.

2 Line a large serving platter with salad greens. Arrange the chick'n in two or three spots atop the greens. Alternatively, arrange the chick'n in overlapping pieces or in a couple of rows.

3 Arrange the celery, pineapple and/ or orange, bell pepper, tomatoes, and cashews in aesthetically pleasing separate mounds on the salad greens.

4 Let guests compose their own plates or compose each plate yourself from the components on the platter. Pass the dressing at the table.

NEW YORK DELI-STYLE PASTA SALAD

SERVES 6 TO 8

HERE'S A PASTA SALAD inspired by the deli-counter classic. This version is as meaty and cheesy as the original but richer in vegetables. Even though only half a pound of pasta is used, it goes a long way. As a potluck dish, this a great choice—it's sturdy and tastes great at room temperature.

8 ounces spiral pasta, such as cavatappi, rotini, or gemelli

1 cup vegan feta or other hard vegan cheese, cut into small dice

6 to 8 plant-based deli slices (bologna-, turkey-, or ham-style), cut into short strips

⅔ cup pimiento-stuffed green olives or pitted and halved brine-cured black olives

½ medium zucchini, cut into ½-inch dice

½ medium red bell pepper, cut into ½-inch dice

1 cup fresh cherry or grape tomatoes, halved

2 scallions, thinly sliced

¼ cup chopped fresh parsley or mixed fresh parsley and dill

⅓ cup bottled or homemade vinaigrette, or more if desired

¼ cup vegan mayonnaise

2 teaspoons prepared yellow mustard

Salt and freshly ground pepper to taste

1 Cook the pasta according to package directions until al dente, then drain. Rinse under cold running water until cool, then drain well again.

2 Meanwhile, combine the cheese, deli slices, olives, zucchini, bell pepper, tomatoes, scallions, and herbs in a serving bowl.

3 When the pasta is drained, add it to the serving bowl along with the vinaigrette. Mix well.

4 Combine the mayonnaise and mustard in a small bowl and whisk until completely blended, then add to the pasta mixture.

5 Taste before adding salt (you may not need any), but do add plenty of freshly ground pepper.

Teriyaki Chick'n Salad,
page 182

COBB SALAD

SERVES 4 TO 6

A QUINTESSENTIALLY AMERICAN DISH, this salad was named for chef Robert Cobb way back in the 1930s. That's impressive staying power for a salad! Its special character comes from the arrangement of ingredients in rows on a bed of greens. Traditional recipes usually include both bacon and chicken; it's easy to swap them out for plant-based versions. Other characteristic ingredients are avocado and tomato—those we can keep—and hard-boiled egg, which is replaced here with white beans or chickpeas. Feel free to use a bottled vinaigrette instead of the homemade version below.

PLANT PROTEIN OPTIONS

Plant-based chick'n chunks

½ recipe Chicken-Style Seitan Cutlets (page 222)

Baked tofu

VARIATION

Mix some baby spinach or several leaves of stemmed, sliced, and massaged kale (see directions on page 188) in with the spring greens or lettuce for extra color and vitamins.

FOR THE DRESSING

⅓ cup extra-virgin olive oil

¼ cup red wine vinegar

1 tablespoon prepared Dijon mustard

1 tablespoon freshly squeezed lemon juice (optional)

1 teaspoon Italian seasoning

FOR THE SALAD

1 tablespoon olive oil or other vegetable oil, divided

8 ounces chicken-style plant protein (see options at left), finely diced or shredded

6 slices plant-based bacon or ½ recipe Smoky Tempeh Strips (page 224), cut into ½-inch pieces

Spring mix or other torn or shredded lettuce to taste

¾ cup canned white beans or chickpeas, drained and rinsed

1 medium ripe avocado, pitted, peeled, and diced

1 cup fresh cherry or grape tomatoes, halved

Thinly sliced scallion or minced chives for garnish

1 Combine the dressing ingredients in a small bowl and whisk, then set aside.

2 Heat ½ tablespoon oil in a medium skillet over medium heat. Add the plant-based chicken and sauté until touched with golden spots here and there, 6 to 8 minutes. Transfer to a plate.

3 Heat the remaining oil in the skillet and sauté the bacon over medium-high heat until lightly browned and crisp, 6 to 8 minutes.

4 Line a serving platter with spring mix or lettuce. Arrange two rows of chick'n over it, a row of bacon, and then a row each of the beans, avocado, and tomatoes.

5 Drizzle a little dressing over the salad or pass it at the table. Sprinkle the salad with scallion or chives and serve at once.

KALE CAESAR SALAD

SERVES 6 TO 8

THE PLANT-BASED FOOD WORLD has messed mightily—but in good ways—with the original Caesar salad, another enduring midcentury American classic. Those of us of the vegan persuasion often add kale to the mix, since all that lettuce by itself is a bit boring: the croutons stay, but a bit of plant-based bacon joins them, along with avocado. Gone is the original dressing made of anchovies, Worcestershire sauce (which also contains anchovies), and raw egg yolks (yikes!); any creamy dressing works well. The result is still a salad of stunning simplicity, and now we can say, "All hail, kale Caesar!"

FOR THE CROUTONS AND BACON

4 to 5 cups diced day-old French or Italian bread

Cooking oil spray to taste

Salt-free seasoning to taste

6 to 8 strips plant-based bacon or ½ recipe Smoky Tempeh Strips (page 224), cut into small bits

SALAD

6 to 8 kale leaves (preferably lacinato), stemmed and thinly sliced

Olive oil for massaging kale

1 large or 2 medium heads romaine lettuce

½ cup Vegan Ranch Dressing (page 238) or any creamy vegan bottled dressing, or as desired

1 medium ripe avocado, pitted, peeled, and diced

Easy Plant Parmesan for topping (page 243; optional)

1 Preheat the oven to 350°F. Line a roasting pan with parchment paper.

2 To make the croutons, spread the bread cubes in the prepared pan. Spray with a little cooking oil spray; sprinkle lightly with seasoning. Stir, then repeat.

3 Add the bacon to the baking sheet and stir. Bake for 15 to 20 minutes, or until the bread is golden, stirring every 5 minutes or so. Remove from the oven and set aside.

4 Meanwhile, put the kale in a mixing bowl. Rub a small amount of olive oil onto your palms and massage the kale leaves for 30 to 60 seconds, until they turn bright green and soften.

5 Cut each head of romaine in half lengthwise, then slice horizontally into ribbons. Add it to the kale and toss.

6 Add enough dressing to generously coat (but not drown) the romaine and kale, stirring until evenly coated.

7 Transfer the lettuce and kale mixture to a large platter or shallow serving bowl. Top with the avocado, followed by the croutons and bacon. Sprinkle with plant Parmesan, if desired, and serve at once.

"TUNA" WALDORF SALAD

SERVES 4

A TRUE AMERICAN CLASSIC, Waldorf salad is a familiar mixture of apples, walnuts, and celery. Adding plant-based tuna makes it more of a main dish. If you can get hold of a loaf of fresh sourdough bread, that's an absolutely fantastic pairing with this salad.

2 medium crisp sweet apples, cored and diced

Juice of ½ lemon

2 large celery stalks, diced

½ cup raisins or dried cranberries

½ cup finely chopped toasted or untoasted walnuts

6 to 8 ounces plant-based tuna, flaked

½ cup vegan mayonnaise, or to taste

Mixed baby greens or chopped lettuce to taste

1 Combine the apples and lemon juice in a mixing bowl and toss. Add the celery, raisins, walnuts, tuna, and mayonnaise and toss well.

2 Line a serving platter with greens and arrange the salad over them. Alternatively, line four individual salad plates or shallow bowls with greens, then divide the salad over them and serve at once.

SPINACH SALAD
WITH APPLE & BACON

SERVES 4 TO 6

THERE'S SOMETHING SO SATISFYING about the contrasting flavors and textures of sweet apple and smoky bacon. Tossed with a bottled raspberry vinaigrette, this lovely salad goes down as easy as candy and is yours in no time. It isn't quite hefty enough to serve as a main-dish salad, so I suggest serving it with a simple vegetable soup and some fresh bread.

VARIATION

This is also nice made with ¼ cup shelled pumpkin seeds (pepitas) instead of the walnuts. If you get them pretoasted, you can skip adding them to the skillet and simply scatter them over the salad along with the bacon.

Vegetable oil or cooking oil spray for the pan

6 slices plant-based bacon or ½ recipe Smoky Tempeh Strips (page 224), cut into small bits

⅓ cup chopped walnuts

2 to 3 ounces baby spinach or a combination of spinach and arugula

½ cup grated carrots

2 medium crisp sweet apples, cored and diced

½ cup bottled raspberry vinaigrette, or to taste

Freshly ground pepper to taste

1 Heat a little olive oil or cooking oil spray in a medium skillet. Add the bacon and cook over medium heat, stirring often, for 5 minutes.

2 Add the walnuts and continue to cook until the bacon is lightly browned and crisp, about 5 minutes longer.

3 Meanwhile, combine the spinach, carrots, apples, and vinaigrette in a mixing bowl and stir.

4 Spread the spinach mixture on a serving platter. Add a few grinds of fresh pepper.

5 Scatter the bacon and walnuts over the spinach mixture, then serve at once.

DECONSTRUCTED
SUSHI BOWL / WITH "TUNA"

SERVES 4 TO 6

IF YOU'VE EVER MADE sushi at home, you know it's quite a project. The results can be amazing with some practice, but what a mess it leaves behind—sticky rice everywhere! If you're a sushi fan with a DIY spirit, though, you might really enjoy the idea of combining the flavors you love in a fuss-free cold dish.

Typical sushi vegetables such as avocado, cucumber, and carrots are added to gingery rice. Plant-based tuna (or plant-based salmon, a.k.a. lox) and nori add the seafood flavor. To make this as easy as can be, I use nori snacks, which come in small packages you can find in the snack aisle of natural foods stores. Two brands to look for are Annie Chun's and Sea Tangle Snacks.

VARIATIONS

Substitute steamed fresh or thawed frozen riced cauliflower for half the rice.

Substitute sliced shiitake mushrooms, very lightly steamed asparagus (cut into very short pieces), thinly sliced radishes, and/or julienned daikon or turnips for the carrots, cucumber, tuna, and/or avocado.

3 to 3½ cups cooked rice (see note), at room temperature

¼ cup rice vinegar, or more if desired

2 tablespoons natural granulated sugar

Pinch of salt

2 teaspoons grated fresh or squeeze-bottle ginger, or more if desired

1 tablespoon sesame or other vegetable oil, or more if desired

1 cup baby carrots, quartered lengthwise, or 1 cup grated carrot

½ medium cucumber, quartered lengthwise and sliced

3 to 4 ounces plant-based tuna, flaked, or plant-based salmon, cut into small bits

1 medium ripe avocado, pitted, peeled, and diced

6 to 8 pieces nori snacks, cut into narrow strips, divided

1 scallion, very thinly sliced

Sesame seeds for garnish (optional)

1 In a mixing bowl, combine the rice with the vinegar, sugar, salt, ginger, and oil. Stir and let stand for a few minutes.

2 Stir the carrot, cucumber, and tuna into the rice. Taste and add more vinegar, ginger, and oil if desired.

3 Just before serving, add the avocado and most of the nori. Scatter the remaining nori and scallion over the top and garnish with sesame seeds (if desired).

NOTE: *You need not use sushi rice in this recipe. White, jasmine, and basmati rice work well, as does short-grain brown rice.*

CHAPTER 8

BREAKFAST & BRUNCH

WHEN IT COMES TO breakfast, two meats seem to rule—bacon and sausage. Being Ms. Avocado Toast myself, I was willfully oblivious to just how prevalent this morning meat habit is in the world at large. That is, until all the recent news broke about how popular plant-based breakfast sausage sandwiches have become at fast-food eateries.

So this chapter kicks off, appropriately, with a recipe that marries two trends—breakfast sausage (which you can buy in ready-made form or make yourself) and avocado—merged into a muffin. In this brief chapter, you'll find a number of hearty dishes featuring plant-based bacon, sausage, and chorizo (with a brief nod to lox—yes, it comes in plant-based form) that will wow your brunch guests and fuel your weekends.

BREAKFAST MUFFINS

SERVES 4

THE ALTERNATIVE BREAKFAST SANDWICHES now being served at fast-food places usually consist of plant-based sausage, cheese, and egg on an English muffin. But alas, usually the cheese and egg aren't of the vegan variety. Still, it's a step in the right direction, and there's movement toward offering this classic breakfast sandwich in all-vegan form.

Here's a breakfast sandwich that's a step up from the traditional sausage (or bacon), egg, and cheese variety. This one uses vegan cheese, of course, and the egg is replaced with a slab of sautéed tofu. A hint of jam, plus avocado and tomato, take it to the next level. If you have a good appetite in the morning, chances are you'll want two! Feel free to use both bacon *and* sausage in this sandwich.

VARIATION

Substitute some baby spinach for the avocado and/or tomato. You don't have to cook it, but it's even better when you wilt it down slightly. Make sure to press out as much liquid from the spinach as you can once it's wilted and use as much as each muffin will comfortably hold.

1 (14-ounce) tub extra-firm tofu

Vegan butter for the pan

Salt and freshly ground pepper to taste

4 English muffins, split or cut open

Apricot or fig jam or orange marmalade to taste

4 slices vegan cheese, any variety

8 strips plant-based bacon, 4 packaged plant-based sausage patties, or 4 Tempeh Breakfast Sausage Patties (page 232)

1 medium ripe avocado, pitted, peeled, and sliced

2 medium ripe fresh tomatoes, thinly sliced

1 Cut the block of tofu into a square roughly the same size as the English muffins. Reserve the excess tofu for another use.

2 Carefully cut the tofu square in half through the thickness to form two equal squares. Blot them very well between paper towels or a clean tea towel.

3 Carefully cut each square of tofu through the thickness again so that you wind up with four fairly even pieces, each about ¼ inch thick.

4 Heat enough vegan butter to coat a medium skillet. When the butter starts to sizzle, add the tofu pieces and cook over medium-high heat until golden and starting to turn crisp, about 4 minutes on each side. Sprinkle with salt and pepper when nearly done.

5 While the tofu is cooking, toast the English muffins, then place one on each of four serving plates. Spread each bottom half with jam, followed by a slice of cheese.

6 When the tofu is done, place one piece over each slice of cheese.

7 Cook the bacon or sausage in the same skillet over medium-high heat, adding a little more vegan butter if necessary, until crisp on both sides. Cut the bacon slices so that they will fit fairly neatly over the tofu slices, then distribute them evenly over the muffins.

8 Arrange avocado and tomato slices over the bacon, then cover with the top halves of the muffins. Serve at once.

SPICY CHORIZO TOFU
SCRAMBLE

SERVES 4

THIS HEARTY, SPICY SCRAMBLE delivers a double dose of protein from tofu and plant-based chorizo. Enjoy this for breakfast or brunch, and it could keep you going until dinnertime! It's delicious served with warmed flour tortillas and fresh fruit. If you opt to use the DIY chorizo for this recipe, it's best to make it before starting.

VARIATION

If you serve this with tortillas, they can simply be used to scoop up some of the scramble, but they can also be used to make soft tacos. Large tortillas can be wrapped around a mound of this scramble to make breakfast burritos.

1 (14-ounce) tub extra-firm tofu

2 tablespoons extra-virgin olive oil, divided

¼ teaspoon curry powder

8 to 10 ounces packaged plant-based chorizo or 1 recipe Tempeh and Mushroom Chorizo (page 215)

1 large onion, quartered and thinly sliced

1 medium red bell pepper, diced

6 to 8 leaves lacinato kale or collard greens, stemmed and cut into ribbons

¼ cup chopped fresh cilantro

Salt and freshly ground pepper to taste

Sriracha or other hot sauce to taste

Soft flour or corn tortillas for serving (optional)

1 Cut the tofu into 6 slabs. Blot well between layers of paper towels or a clean tea towel. Cut the slabs into approximately ½-inch dice.

2 Heat 1 tablespoon oil in a large skillet or stir-fry pan. Add the tofu and sauté over medium-high heat for 2 to 3 minutes before sprinkling in the curry powder (which is mainly for color).

3 If using packaged chorizo, add it to the pan and continue to cook, stirring often, until both it and the tofu start turning golden and crisp here and there, about 8 minutes longer. Transfer to a plate or bowl. If using Tempeh and Mushroom Chorizo, add it to the tofu.

4 Heat the remaining oil in the same pan. Add the onion and sauté over medium heat until golden. Add the bell pepper and greens and continue to sauté until all are crisp-tender, about 5 minutes.

5 Return the tofu-chorizo mixture to the pan and stir.

6 Add the cilantro and season with salt and pepper. Continue to cook until everything is well heated through. Add the sriracha or pass it at the table, along with tortillas (if desired).

DENVER
TOFU SCRAMBLE

SERVES 3 TO 4

THE TRIO OF INGREDIENTS that are always part of a Denver omelet—onion, bell pepper, and ham—are featured in this easy and tasty tofu scramble. In this case, you don't have to scour the markets for plant-based ham, which isn't as common as other kinds of deli slices; any variety will do quite well. Serve with fresh fruit and whole-grain toast for a hearty breakfast or brunch.

1 (14-ounce) tub firm or extra-firm tofu

1 tablespoon extra-virgin olive oil or vegan butter

1 large onion, quartered and thinly sliced

1 medium bell pepper, any color, cut into short, narrow strips

½ teaspoon curry powder, or more to taste

8 plant-based deli slices, preferably ham-style, cut into short, narrow strips

1 medium fresh ripe tomato, finely diced

2 scallions, thinly sliced

Salt and freshly ground pepper to taste

1 cup vegan cheese shreds, any style (optional)

Sriracha or other hot sauce for serving (optional)

1 Cut the tofu into 5 or 6 slices horizontally and blot well between layers of paper towels or a clean tea towel. Set aside.

2 Heat the oil in a medium skillet. Add the onion and sauté over medium heat until translucent. Add the bell pepper and continue to sauté until both are golden, about 5 minutes, or continue to cook until both are lightly browned, if you like.

3 Crumble the tofu into the skillet and sprinkle in the curry powder. Mix well.

4 Add the deli slices, tomato, scallions, and salt and pepper. Cook over medium-high heat for 6 to 8 minutes, stirring frequently.

5 Stir in the vegan cheese shreds, if desired. Serve immediately, passing hot sauce at the table.

SCRAMBLED TOFU & SAUSAGE BREAKFAST BURRITOS

SERVES 6 **WELCOME THE WEEKEND WITH** these easy burritos, stuffed generously with scrambled tofu and plant-based sausage (the kind you buy or the kind you make). While these are fantastic for breakfast or brunch, there's no reason why you couldn't serve them for a quick lunch or dinner. A salad—of either the fruit or vegetable variety (or both)—is all you need to complete the meal.

1 (14-ounce) tub firm or extra-firm tofu

2 tablespoons extra-virgin olive oil or vegan butter, divided

4 small packaged plant-based sausage patties or 4 Tempeh Breakfast Sausage Patties (page 232), crumbled

1 cup prepared salsa

¼ teaspoon curry powder

2 scallions, thinly sliced

¼ cup chopped fresh cilantro (optional)

1½ cups Cheddar- or pepper Jack–style vegan cheese shreds

6 (10-inch) soft flour tortillas

1 Cut the tofu into 6 slabs. Blot well between layers of paper towels or a clean tea towel. Cut the slabs into ½-inch dice. Set aside.

2 Heat 1 tablespoon oil in a medium skillet. Cook the crumbled sausage over medium-high heat until lightly browned, stirring often. Transfer to a bowl and cover.

3 Heat the remaining oil in the same skillet over medium heat. Add the tofu, salsa, curry powder (which is mostly for color), scallions, and cilantro, if desired. Cook over medium heat for 3 to 4 minutes, until well heated through. Increase the heat and cook a little longer if there's liquid in the skillet that needs to evaporate. Stir in the cheese and remove from the heat.

4 Divide the scrambled tofu mixture among the tortillas, arranging it in the center of each in an oblong shape and leaving room at each end.

5 Divide the sausage among the tortillas, arranging it next to the tofu mixture.

6 Fold two ends over the tofu mixture, then roll up the rest. Repeat with each burrito. Cut the burritos in half or leave them whole. Either way, serve at once.

TOFU QUICHE

WITH BACON OR LOX

SERVES 6

TOFU QUICHE HAS BEEN around for a while as an alternative to the classic variety, made with eggs. This version isn't intended to fool anyone, though no one will miss the eggs. It's packed with vegetables and spiked with bits of plant-based bacon. There's also an option to include one of vegan cuisine's newest innovations, plant-based smoked salmon (lox).

VEGETABLE OPTIONS

Use about 1½ cups steamed or sautéed vegetables for a regular pie or 2 cups for a deep-dish pie. A combination of two vegetables is ideal. Here are some ideas:

Asparagus: Bottoms trimmed, cut into 2-inch lengths, and lightly steamed

Broccoli: Finely chopped and lightly steamed

Bell peppers: Cut into strips and sautéed in olive oil until lightly browned

Mushrooms: Cleaned, stemmed, and chopped

Spinach or baby greens: 1 (5-ounce) package, rinsed, wilted, and chopped

---

1½ tablespoons extra-virgin olive oil

1½ cups chopped onion

2 cloves garlic, minced

1 (14-ounce) tub firm tofu, well blotted and coarsely crumbled

1 teaspoon curry powder

1½ to 2 cups mixed steamed or sautéed vegetables of your choice (see options at left)

2 to 4 tablespoons chopped fresh herbs, such as parsley, dill, chives, and/or cilantro

4 to 5 ounces plant-based bacon or vegan smoked salmon (lox), cut into small bits

Salt and freshly ground pepper to taste

1 (9-inch) good-quality vegan pastry crust, preferably whole-grain

⅓ cup bread crumbs for topping (optional)

---

1 Preheat the oven to 350°F.

2 Heat the oil in a wide skillet. Add the onion and sauté until golden. Add the garlic and continue to sauté until the onion turns golden brown. Remove from the heat.

3 Transfer half the onion mixture to a food processor along with the tofu and curry powder and process until smooth.

4 In a mixing bowl, combine the blended tofu with the remaining onion mixture. Add the vegetables, herbs, and bacon or lox. Season with salt and pepper and mix thoroughly.

5 Pour the mixture into the crust and pat with your hands to smooth. Top with the bread crumbs, if desired.

6 Bake for 40 minutes, or until set. Let stand for 10 minutes or so, then cut into wedges and serve.

TWO-POTATO & CHORIZO
HASH BROWNS

SERVES 4 TO 6

I FIND HEARTY HASH-BROWN skillets irresistible, and this one goes an extra mile or two by adding sweet potatoes, greens, and plant-based chorizo. If there's any lingering myth that vegan fare is rabbit food, dishes like this help put it to rest! Like many of the hearty brunch dishes in this chapter, all you need to complete the meal is fresh bread or tortillas and a simple salad or fruit.

2 to 3 medium-large yellow or red-skinned potatoes

1 to 2 medium-large sweet potatoes

2 tablespoons extra-virgin olive oil, divided

1 medium onion, finely chopped

1 medium zucchini, cut in ½-inch dice

2 cups chopped green cabbage or kale

1 (8- to 10-ounce) package plant-based chorizo or 1 recipe Tempeh and Mushroom Chorizo (page 215)

1 teaspoon sweet or smoked paprika, or more to taste

Salt and freshly ground pepper to taste

¼ cup chopped fresh parsley or cilantro, or more to taste, divided

1 Scrub the potatoes and microwave them, starting at 1 minute per potato, until they're about half done. You should be able to pierce through them, but with a lot of resistance. Microwave the sweet potatoes separately to make sure that neither they nor the other potatoes get overcooked. When the potatoes and sweet potatoes are cool enough to handle, peel them, if desired, and cut them into ½-inch dice.

2 Heat 1 tablespoon oil in a large skillet. Add the onion and sauté over medium heat until translucent. Add the diced potatoes and continue to sauté, stirring often, until they and the onion are lightly browned, 10 to 12 minutes.

3 Add the zucchini and cabbage or kale and sauté for 2 to 3 minutes longer, or just until crisp-tender. Transfer to a plate or bowl and cover.

4 Heat the remaining oil in the skillet. If using packaged chorizo, sauté the chorizo over medium-high heat for about 8 minutes, or until lightly browned, breaking up larger chunks with a wooden spoon or spatula.

5 Return the vegetable mixture to the skillet. If using Tempeh and Mushroom Chorizo, add it to the skillet now too. Stir gently and heat through.

6 Season with paprika, salt, and pepper. Stir in most of the parsley and top with the remainder. Serve at once.

BISCUITS
WITH SAUSAGE GRAVY

SERVES 4

SOUTHERN-STYLE BISCUITS ARE USUALLY made with butter and buttermilk—of the dairy variety—and the sausages are usually made with ... well, there's a reason behind that saying about not wanting to know how sausage gets made.

In our case, we know how vegan sausage gets made because *all* the ingredients are listed right on the package. You also have the option of making the DIY sausages on page 230. The recipe for the biscuits was provided by this book's photographer, Hannah Kaminsky.

No matter what sausage option you go with, it's a kinder, gentler version of an American classic. As someone who has never had the "other" kind of biscuits with sausage gravy and didn't quite get the appeal on paper, I find this to be freaking delicious and hope you will, too!

FOR THE BASIC FLAKY BISCUITS

2 cups unbleached all-purpose flour

1 tablespoon natural granulated sugar

1 tablespoon baking powder

¼ teaspoon baking soda

¼ teaspoon salt

½ cup vegan butter

¾ cup plain unsweetened plant-based milk

1 teaspoon apple cider vinegar

FOR THE SAUSAGE GRAVY

1 tablespoon vegan butter or extra-virgin olive oil

1 small onion, finely chopped

2 links packaged vegan sausage or 1 recipe Savory Sausage (page 230), finely chopped

4 ounces cremini (baby bella) or white mushrooms, cleaned, stemmed, and chopped

3 tablespoons unbleached all-purpose flour

1 cup vegetable broth or 1 regular-size vegetable bouillon cube dissolved in 1 cup water

½ cup plain unsweetened plant-based milk

2 tablespoons nutritional yeast

½ teaspoon dried thyme

½ teaspoon rubbed sage (optional)

Salt and freshly ground pepper to taste

¼ cup finely chopped fresh parsley and/or thinly sliced scallions

Recipe continues

1 Preheat the oven to 450°F. Line a baking sheet with parchment paper or a silicone baking mat.

2 To make the biscuits, whisk the flour, sugar, baking powder, baking soda, and salt in a large bowl. Cut the butter into small cubes and toss them in, coating them with the dry ingredients. Using a pastry cutter, two forks, or your fingers, cut the butter in, working the mixture lightly until it's the consistency of coarse crumbs. The remaining pieces of butter should be no larger than the size of peas.

3 In a separate bowl, combine the plant-based milk and vinegar, then slowly pour into the bowl of dry ingredients. Mix until just incorporated, being careful not to overwork the dough.

4 Turn the dough out onto a well-floured surface and pat down roughly into a rectangle. Fold the dough in half and pat down flat again. Repeat four or five times to create flaky layers.

5 After the final fold, roll the dough out to about 1 inch thick and use a 2½-inch round cookie cutter to cut the biscuits. To keep the layers separate, pull straight up on the cookie cutter—do not twist. Gather up the scraps, press together, and repeat until all the dough is used. Alternatively, instead of the cookie cutter, you can use a very sharp knife to simply slice the dough into 8 equal squares.

6 Place the biscuits on the prepared baking sheet about 1½ inches apart and bake for 12 to 15 minutes, or until golden brown all over. Let cool for at least 15 minutes before serving.

7 Prepare the gravy while the biscuits are cooling. Heat the butter in a medium saucepan. Add the onion and sauté over medium heat until translucent.

8 Add the sausage and mushrooms and continue to sauté until all are golden.

9 Sprinkle the flour into the saucepan and stir. Pour the broth in slowly, stirring constantly to avoid lumping. Stir in the plant-based milk and nutritional yeast and cook until the mixture thickens.

10 Remove from the heat and stir in the thyme and sage, if desired. Season with salt and pepper. If the gravy seems too dense, stir in a little more plant-based milk.

11 To serve, split each biscuit open and slather the bottom halves with gravy. Top with a sprinkling of fresh parsley and/or scallions. Serve hot.

12 Once completely cool, the biscuits can be stored in an airtight container at room temperature for up to five days or frozen for up to four months. To reheat, warm in a 350°F oven for about 10 minutes.

CHEESE GRITS
WITH BACON AND/OR SHRIMP

SERVES 4

CHEESE GRITS ARE, LIKE biscuits and gravy, a southern classic. But I embraced cheese grits early on in my culinary journey—which I never did with biscuits and gravy. Somehow, vegan cheese grits got on our regular rotation when my kids, who liked mushy things, were young.

For anyone unfamiliar with them, grits are basically a coarser version of cornmeal mush. Shrimp and grits, as I've come to find out, is also a southern classic, especially as a brunch dish. Never having been one for shrimp myself, even before I went vegan, the appeal was lost on me. Poking around to find out more about the original seafood-based version of this dish, I learned that it delivers a whopping amount of cholesterol and fat.

I presented a gentle introduction to plant-based shrimp as an option in the recipe for Jambalaya (page 46), and if you want to serve something a little different for brunch, give this recipe a whirl. If plant-based seafood isn't your cup of tea, simply omit the shrimp. And if you do, omit the lemon juice as well.

VARIATION

Add 1 to 1½ cups cooked fresh or thawed frozen corn kernels to the grits along with the tomatoes and scallions.

FOR THE GRITS
4 cups water

1 cup corn grits or coarse cornmeal, preferably stone-ground

FOR THE TOPPING
2 tablespoons extra-virgin olive oil

4 to 5 strips plant-based bacon or ½ recipe Smoky Tempeh Strips (page 224), cut into small bits

1 (8.8-ounce) package breaded plant-based shrimp (optional)

2 to 3 cloves garlic, thinly sliced

2 small fresh ripe tomatoes, diced

2 scallions, thinly sliced, plus more for topping (optional)

Juice of ½ lemon (optional)

1½ tablespoons vegan butter

1 cup Cheddar- or pepper Jack–style vegan cheese shreds

Salt and freshly ground pepper to taste

Recipe continues

1 To make the grits, bring the water to a gentle simmer in a large saucepan. Slowly whisk in the grits, stirring constantly to avoid lumps. Cook gently over low heat for 20 to 25 minutes, or until tender and thick, stirring occasionally. Alternatively, cook the grits according to package directions.

2 To make the topping, heat the oil in a large skillet or stir-fry pan over medium heat. Add the bacon and sauté for 3 to 4 minutes, stirring often.

3 Add the shrimp (if desired) and garlic and continue to sauté for 5 minutes or so, until everything is nicely heated and touched with golden brown.

4 Stir in the tomatoes and scallions and continue to sauté for just a minute or two longer, until both are slightly wilted. Drizzle in the lemon juice (if you're including shrimp).

5 When the grits are done, stir in the vegan butter and cheese. Cook for another minute or two, until the cheese is fairly well melted. Season with salt and pepper.

6 Distribute the grits among four wide shallow bowls and top with the bacon-and-shrimp mixture. If desired, top with extra scallions. Serve at once.

CHAPTER 9
DIY PLANT PROTEINS

THOUGH MANY OF THE recipes in this book showcase convenient packaged, ready-made plant proteins, this concise selection of homemade plant proteins will appeal to those who enjoy a do-it-yourself approach. You'll find options for using them throughout this book.

The recipes aren't complicated. They use whole-foods ingredients such as beans, nuts, tofu, seitan, and others. These preparations are also for you if you want to use plant proteins that are relatively unprocessed and for which *you* control the sodium content.

In this chapter, you'll find a slew of ways to make meaty crumbles, meatballs, and burgers; you'll work on mastering homemade seitan; you'll even learn how sausage (and sausage patties) get made, minus the part that no one wants to know! Even though I love convenience and shortcuts as much as the next busy cook, I had a lot of fun concocting these plant protein analogs and hope you'll enjoy making and using them as well.

TEMPEH & WALNUT GROUND

MAKES ABOUT 3 CUPS

TWO HIGH-PROTEIN FOODS—TEMPEH AND walnuts—team up to make a tasty plant-based ground. Walnuts, by the way, are one of the best, and really one of the only significant, sources of plant-based omega-3 fatty acids. These are among the beneficial "good fats" that are most abundant in seafood. So it's nice to know that there's a plant food that's a rich source of such a valuable nutrient. This tempeh and walnut ground is a fantastic filling for beefy tacos and for boosting protein and adding texture to any bean dish, chili, or stew.

1 tablespoon extra-virgin olive oil

1 medium onion, chopped

1 medium red or green bell pepper, diced

1 (8-ounce) package tempeh

1 cup walnut pieces

1 (15- to 16-ounce) can tomato sauce

1 tablespoon good-quality chili powder

1 tablespoon sweet paprika

1 teaspoon ground cumin

Salt and freshly ground pepper to taste

1 Heat the oil in a large skillet. Add the onion and sauté over medium heat until translucent. Add the bell pepper and continue to sauté until the onion is lightly browned, 6 to 8 minutes.

2 Cut the block of tempeh into a few chunks. Place in a food processor and pulse a few times. Add the walnut pieces and the onion and pepper mixture and pulse until everything is finely and evenly chopped. Be careful not to overprocess—you don't want to turn this into a puree.

3 Transfer the mixture to the same skillet. Add the tomato sauce, chili powder, paprika, cumin, and salt and pepper. Stir and bring to a gentle simmer over medium-high heat. Lower the heat and cook for 15 to 20 minutes to allow the flavors to heighten and blend, stirring often.

4 Serve straight from the skillet, or cool and store for future use. This keeps in the refrigerator in a well-sealed container for up to four days. It freezes well, too.

TEMPEH & MUSHROOM
CHORIZO

MAKES ABOUT 2 CUPS

CHORIZO, A HIGHLY SEASONED chopped or ground sausage, is now easy to find in plant-based versions. And the packaged brands that are available are quite good. But if you're exploring this chapter, chances are you have a DIY spirit, and you'll be delighted by how easy and fast it is to make your own vegan chorizo. Tempeh is the perfect base for it, and you can boost the spice level to your liking using the amounts given below as a base. Chorizo is meant to be spicy and smoky, but feel free to adjust the paprika and hot sauce to your comfort level.

1 (8-ounce) package tempeh

1 cup cleaned, stemmed, and coarsely chopped cremini (baby bella) mushrooms

1 tablespoon extra-virgin olive oil

¼ cup very finely chopped onion

¾ cup bottled barbecue sauce or Quick No-Cook Barbecue Sauce (page 240), or more to taste

1 tablespoon smoked paprika or barbecue seasoning, or more to taste

2 teaspoons chili powder

1 teaspoon dried oregano

2 teaspoons sriracha or other hot sauce, or to taste

1 Cut the block of tempeh into a few chunks. Combine the tempeh and mushrooms in a food processor and pulse until the mixture is reduced to crumbles. Take care not to overdo it—you don't want to wind up with a puree.

2 Heat the oil in a medium skillet. Add the onion and sauté over medium heat until golden. Add the tempeh mixture and continue to sauté until it turns golden here and there, stirring occasionally.

3 Add the barbecue sauce, paprika, chili powder, and oregano. Continue to cook until the mixture begins to brown lightly, turning it over frequently, about 10 minutes.

4 Remove from the heat and season with hot sauce and additional paprika, if desired.

5 Store leftovers in the refrigerator in a well-sealed container for up to four days, or freeze for later use.

WALNUT, GRAIN & MUSHROOM CRUMBLES

BEEF-TEXTURED CRUMBLES ARE SO easy to make from whole foods. This one, like the Tempeh and Walnut Ground (page 214), features walnuts, a vegan's go-to source of valuable omega-3 fatty acids. For the crumble effect, you have the option of using bulgur or quinoa. Use the latter if you want to keep this gluten-free, and make sure to use gluten-free soy sauce in that case. Nicely seasoned and deliciously moist, thanks to the mushrooms, this is super tasty in its own right, not necessarily as a dead ringer (excuse the metaphor) for ground beef.

In addition, these crumbles work great as a taco or burrito filling made with the salsa option and are fantastic as a sloppy joe filling with the tomato sauce option. Basically, if you're going Tex-Mex, use the salsa; if you're going Italian, use the tomato sauce.

STORAGE TIP

This keeps in the refrigerator in a well-sealed container for up to four days. It freezes well, too.

¾ cup uncooked bulgur or quinoa

1 tablespoon dried onion flakes

3 to 3½ cups water, divided

1 heaping cup brown mushrooms, cleaned, stemmed, and roughly chopped

¾ cup walnut pieces

1½ tablespoons soy sauce

1½ tablespoons maple syrup

¼ cup good-quality natural ketchup

2 tablespoons barbecue seasoning or 1 (1.5-ounce) packet taco seasoning

1 cup prepared salsa or tomato sauce, divided

1. Combine the grain, onion flakes, and 2 cups water in a medium skillet. Bring to a slow boil, then lower the heat and cover. Simmer until the water is absorbed, about 15 minutes. If the grain isn't done to your liking, add ½ cup more water and cook until absorbed.

2. Meanwhile, combine the mushrooms and walnuts in a food processor and pulse until they're broken up into tiny pieces. Don't overdo it—you don't want to end up with a puree.

3. Add the mushroom and walnut mixture to the skillet along with 1 cup water and the soy sauce, maple syrup, ketchup, and barbecue seasoning. Return to a simmer, then cook over medium heat until the water is absorbed, about 10 minutes.

4. Stir in ½ cup salsa or tomato sauce, then increase the heat to medium-high. Cook until the bottom of the mixture browns lightly, then stir; continue to do this until the entire mixture is touched with golden-brown spots here and there, 8 to 10 minutes.

5. Stir in the remaining salsa or tomato sauce, cook for a minute or so longer, then remove from the heat.

TERIYAKI-FLAVORED
GROUND / WITH A MEATBALL VARIATION

MAKES ABOUT 3 CUPS

HERE'S A NIFTY WAY to make a beefy ground with an Asian spin. A trio of high-protein foods—quinoa, walnuts, and black beans—form the base, flavored with teriyaki or any prepared Asian sauce of your choice. But you need not limit yourself to Asian-style dishes; this preparation makes terrific Italian-style meatballs, too.

VARIATION

Add 1 cup fine bread crumbs to the food processor along with the walnuts. After processing, shape into 1-inch balls and arrange on a parchment-lined baking pan. Spray the meatballs with cooking oil spray to give them a crisp finish. Bake at 350°F for 20 to 25 minutes, carefully turning them once or twice during baking, until golden on most sides. These meatballs can also be sautéed in a wide skillet using just enough oil to coat the surface, turning them gently until golden and crisp all over.

Korean barbecue sauce, which has become widely available in the Asian foods aisles of well-stocked supermarkets, can be used in place of teriyaki sauce. Asian black bean sauce works, too.

- 1½ tablespoons neutral vegetable oil (such as safflower) or sesame oil, divided
- 1 small onion, finely chopped
- 2 to 3 cloves garlic, minced
- ⅓ cup uncooked quinoa, preferably red
- ¾ cup water
- ⅓ cup chopped walnuts
- 1 cup cooked or canned black beans, drained and rinsed
- ½ cup bottled teriyaki sauce or homemade Teriyaki Sauce (page 241)
- 2 tablespoons hemp seeds (optional)
- 1 teaspoon sriracha or other hot sauce, or more to taste

1 Heat 1 tablespoon oil in a small saucepan. Add the onion and sauté over medium-low heat until translucent. Add the garlic and continue to sauté until both are golden.

2 Add the quinoa and water to the saucepan. Bring to a slow boil, then lower the heat, cover, and cook until the water is absorbed, about 15 minutes.

3 Place the walnuts in a food processor and pulse until nearly powdered. Add the beans and pulse until they're finely chopped.

4 Add the quinoa and onion mixture to the food processor along with the teriyaki sauce, hemp seeds, if desired, and sriracha. Pulse until everything is well blended.

5 Heat the remaining oil in a medium skillet. Add the quinoa mixture and cook over medium-high heat until sizzling hot and starting to brown, about 10 minutes, stirring frequently. Add more teriyaki sauce if desired.

6 Store leftovers in the refrigerator in a well-sealed container for up to four days, or freeze for later use.

TRADITIONAL
BEEF-STYLE SEITAN

**MAKES ABOUT
2 POUNDS**

WHEN IT COMES TO packaged seitan, it can range from shoe-leather tough to middling to quite good. But I've never found one product I can go straight to calling great. Since I use it pretty regularly, I've gotten into the habit of making my own once a month or so. Gluten flour makes it so easy.

I've been tweaking this simple formula for years, and though you'll find a number of variations in books and around the Web—incorporating chickpea flour, nut flours, flavorings, beans, and other ingredients (we'll get a taste of those in the Chicken-Style Seitan Cutlets on page 222)—it's good to nail this basic recipe first. Then by all means experiment as much as you wish.

I like the tender, flavorful seitan that results from this recipe; one of the secrets to its success is the addition of baking powder. I also like the generous yield. Often, I'll freeze half of it—it's always nice to come across it a week or two later.

STORAGE TIP

Once it has cooled, transfer whatever portion of seitan you won't be using right away to a container, then pour in enough of the cooking broth to cover. Use within a few days or freeze. A day or two before you plan to use the frozen portions, thaw the whole container in your refrigerator.

FOR THE DOUGH

2 tablespoons soy sauce, tamari, or Bragg Liquid Aminos

1 cup water, plus more if necessary

2¼ cups gluten flour (vital wheat gluten)

1 teaspoon baking powder

2 tablespoons nutritional yeast (optional)

FOR THE COOKING BROTH

1 large or 2 regular-size vegetable bouillon cubes

2 tablespoons soy sauce, tamari, or Bragg Liquid Aminos

3 to 4 slices fresh ginger or 1 tablespoon squeeze-bottle ginger

1 Combine the soy sauce and water in a small mixing bowl and stir.

2 Combine the gluten flour, baking powder, and nutritional yeast in a medium mixing bowl.

3 Gradually add the water and soy sauce mixture to the dry ingredients to form a stiff dough, stirring with a spoon at first, then working together with your hands. Drizzle in a little more water if necessary; you want all the dry ingredients to be moistened while making sure the dough remains stiff.

4 Turn out onto a floured board (you can use more gluten flour for this) and knead for 2 to 3 minutes. It's not going to be completely smooth, but really work it!

Recipe continues

5 Return the dough to a bowl, then cover with a clean tea towel. Let it rest for 15 minutes.

6 Meanwhile, fill a large soup pot about two-thirds full with water. Add the bouillon cubes, soy sauce, and ginger. Heat over medium-high heat.

7 Once the dough has rested, divide it into two more or less equal pieces and pull each one into a long, narrow loaf, the shape of a miniature baguette. This dough isn't easy to work with; it tends to spring back to whatever shape it's in, but do the best you can—it will come out fine.

8 With a sharp serrated knife, cut each section of dough into slices no thicker than ½ inch each.

9 When the water comes to a slow boil, gently drop in the dough slices. Within a couple of minutes, the dough will puff up and look like it wants to escape the cooking pot. Keep pushing the pieces down into the water; it will settle back. I like to reach in with kitchen shears and cut pieces that have expanded crazily, but this is optional.

10 Simmer gently and steadily, uncovered, for 30 minutes. Remove the pieces with a slotted spoon and set on a plate or cutting board until cool enough to handle. When cool, cut into smaller slices or chunks. Save some of the tasty cooking broth to use in soups, stews, and gravies.

CHICKEN-STYLE
SEITAN CUTLETS

**MAKES ABOUT 2
POUNDS**

THESE CUTLETS ARE FIRMER and flatter than Traditional Beef-Style Seitan pieces (page 219). They can be sliced into strips for stir-fries or chopped into bite-size pieces for salads. You can also make impressive fried or grilled cutlets with them (see the serving suggestion below).

The possibilities are endless for this easy homemade chicken substitute made from gluten and chickpeas, and I recommend them many times throughout these chapters. Make sure to use chickpeas that are plump and tender for best results.

SERVING SUGGESTION

Carefully slice four of the cutlets in half through the thickness. Combine ¼ cup fine cornmeal, ½ teaspoon Italian seasoning, a pinch of salt, and some freshly ground pepper in a shallow bowl and stir. Transfer to a plate. Pour ¼ cup liquid from the canned chickpeas into the bowl. Dip each cutlet in the chickpea liquid, then dredge on both sides with the cornmeal mixture.

Heat enough oil or vegan butter to coat a wide skillet over medium-high heat. When it's nice and hot, sauté the cutlets on both sides until golden and crisp. Serve with Mushroom Gravy (page 245) or even Sausage Gravy (page 207).

- 1 cup canned chickpeas, drained and rinsed, liquid reserved
- 2 tablespoons extra-virgin olive oil or neutral vegetable oil (such as safflower)
- 1¾ cups gluten flour (vital wheat gluten)
- 2 tablespoons nutritional yeast (optional)
- 1 teaspoon baking powder
- 2 teaspoons poultry seasoning
- Vegetable broth for steaming

1 Preheat the oven to 350°F.

2 Put the chickpeas in a food processor. Pour the liquid from the can into a measuring cup and add enough water to make 1 cup. Add this to the food processor and puree until smooth. Add the olive oil, gluten flour, nutritional yeast (if desired), baking powder, and poultry seasoning and process until the mixture holds together in a smooth ball of soft dough.

3 Transfer the dough to a floured cutting board and form it into a thick log. Divide into 8 more or less equal pieces using a sharp serrated knife. Press each slice between your palms to flatten into cutlets, at most ½ inch thick.

4 Arrange the pieces in a single layer in one or two shallow baking dishes, then pour in about ½ inch of broth. Cover with lids or with foil.

5 Bake for 30 minutes, then turn the cutlets over and replenish the broth. Bake for 20 minutes longer.

6 Remove from the oven and let cool until just warm or at room temperature; they'll be easier to slice and handle. Store leftovers in the refrigerator in a well-sealed container for up to four days, or freeze for later use.

SMOKY TEMPEH STRIPS

MAKES ABOUT 16 STRIPS

THIS RECIPE OFFERS AN easy way to make homemade bacon using high-protein tempeh. Slightly sweet, smoky, and savory, these strips come together quickly and, to my palate, taste better than commercially prepared tempeh bacon. They're good for more than just breakfast, too: you can use them in sandwiches and wraps, as a topping for dishes of all sorts, including soups and grain bowls, and even as a high-protein side dish. They're a perfect companion to tofu scrambles, for example.

One caveat: you'll need a good nonstick pan. Because of the syrup, you could wind up with a sticky mess otherwise, which I learned the hard way. If you don't own such a pan, no worries! You can use the oven-roasting option and protect your pan with a layer of parchment paper.

STORAGE TIP

Leftovers can be stored in a tightly covered container in the refrigerator for up to four days.

- 1 (8-ounce) package tempeh, any variety
- 2 tablespoons soy sauce
- 1 tablespoon extra-virgin olive oil or neutral vegetable oil (such as safflower)
- 2 tablespoons good-quality natural ketchup
- 2 tablespoons maple or agave syrup
- Sriracha or other hot sauce to taste
- 2 teaspoons barbecue seasoning or smoked paprika

1 Cut the block of tempeh crosswise into strips no thicker than ¼ inch. Set aside.

2 Combine the remaining ingredients in a small bowl and stir.

3 **To cook in a skillet:** Heat the soy sauce mixture in a wide nonstick skillet. Arrange the tempeh strips in the skillet and turn them over right away so that both sides get coated. Cook over medium-low heat until the tempeh starts to brown lightly on one side, 4 to 5 minutes, then turn over again to brown the second side, about 4 minutes longer, or until all the sauce is absorbed.

4 Reduce the heat to low and continue to sauté until the sauce envelops the tempeh nicely. If necessary, cover the skillet to avoid splatter.

5 **To bake:** Preheat the oven to 400ºF. Line a baking pan with parchment paper. Pour in the soy sauce mixture, then add the tempeh strips in a single layer. Turn them over so that both sides get coated. Cover the pan with foil.

6 Bake for 15 minutes, then turn the strips over. Move them around a bit to ensure that they absorb the sauce. Cover again and bake for 10 to 15 minutes longer, until the sauce is absorbed and the strips are nicely roasted. Serve warm or at room temperature.

CRAZY EASY
CHICKPEA
CHICK'N

**MAKES ABOUT
1½ CUPS**

I GOT THIS IDEA from one of my BFFs, who likes to have sautéed chickpeas for breakfast. Indeed, I discovered that light browning transforms this tasty legume's mouth feel in an unexpected way. Use it in recipes calling for chopped chicken or as a filling for wraps and sandwiches. It's especially good in the Chick'n Pot Pie Casserole (page 40) and the "Tuna" Melts (page 135). Make it anytime you prefer a DIY protein to the kinds that come ready-made.

1 (15-ounce) can chickpeas, drained, 2 tablespoons liquid reserved

1 tablespoon extra-virgin olive oil or neutral vegetable oil (such as safflower)

1 teaspoon poultry seasoning

2 tablespoons nutritional yeast

¼ cup vegan mayonnaise

1 Coarsely mash the chickpeas on a plate or shallow bowl. You may see a lot of the little skins getting loose, but they'll disappear during the cooking process.

2 Heat the oil in a small skillet. Add the chickpeas and sauté over medium-high heat, stirring occasionally, until nicely golden brown here and there, about 10 minutes.

3 Stir in the reserved chickpea liquid, poultry seasoning, and nutritional yeast, then add the mayonnaise a tablespoon at a time until it disappears into the mixture. Continue to sauté for just a minute or so longer, then remove from the heat.

4 Serve warm or at room temperature.

PLANT-POWERED
MEATBALLS

I'VE MADE THESE WITH great success using all the options listed in this recipe—lentils, beans, tempeh, and plant-based ground. If using the latter, make sure to use ground rather than crumbles, which will result in meatballs that are, not surprisingly, crumbly. The other options will result in moist yet firm meatballs that hold together nicely in recipes.

STORAGE TIP

Store leftovers in an airtight container in the refrigerator, where they'll keep for 3 days. These freeze well, too. Thaw in the refrigerator, then sauté on the stovetop or heat in a medium oven.

1 tablespoon extra-virgin olive oil

1 medium onion, finely chopped

3 cloves garlic, minced

1 slice fresh whole-grain bread, torn into a few pieces

1 tablespoon barbecue seasoning

2 teaspoons sweet or smoked paprika

1 teaspoon Italian seasoning

1½ cups cooked or canned lentils or red beans, crumbled tempeh, or plant-based ground

1 cup quick-cooking oats

½ cup unbleached all-purpose or pastry flour or almond meal

½ cup prepared barbecue sauce or Korean barbecue sauce

2 tablespoons nutritional yeast (optional)

Freshly ground pepper to taste

Cooking oil spray (optional)

1 Preheat the oven to 350°F. Line a baking sheet with parchment paper.

2 Heat the oil in a small skillet. Add the onion and sauté over medium heat until translucent. Add the garlic and continue to sauté until both are golden, about 5 minutes. Remove from the heat.

3 Place the bread in a food processor and pulse until finely crumbled.

4 Add the onion mixture, followed by the barbecue seasoning, paprika, Italian seasoning, lentils, oats, flour, barbecue sauce, nutritional yeast (if desired), and pepper, and pulse until well blended, being careful not to overprocess—leave a little texture.

5 Scoop the mixture out by rounded tablespoons, roll into balls with your hands, and arrange on the prepared baking sheet. For a crisp texture, spray the meatballs with cooking oil spray, if desired, before placing in the oven.

6 Bake for 10 to 12 minutes, or until golden on the underside. Turn over and bake for 10 minutes longer, or until the other side is golden as well. Serve right away on pasta or in another preparation.

HOMEMADE BURGERS:
A SIMPLE TEMPLATE

MAKES 6 LARGE OR 8
TO 9 SMALL PATTIES

THESE HEARTY BURGERS WERE inspired by my friend and colleague Laura Theodore, also known as the Jazzy Vegetarian. (That's her brand, though she's a longtime vegan.) Her famous Hungry Guy Burgers, using only five ingredients, proved to me that homemade vegan burgers don't need to contain a million ingredients and require lots of preparation to be really good.

This template calls for beans and plant-based ground combined with an intensely flavored sauce, which I call a flavor bomb. Substitute lentils for the beans, or vary the kind of beans you use, to give the burgers a different character each time you make them. You can also vary the kind of prepared sauce you use for the flavor bomb.

What's the advantage of making burgers at home, with all the great ready-made plant-based burgers available? For one, homemade burgers are more economical. You wind up with a large quantity of burgers for a big family or hungry eaters who might like a second helping. It's also a great way to make food for the weeks ahead, since these freeze quite well.

Finally, because these are so easy to make, it can simply be fun when you have the time to spare. While these are baking, roast some vegetables or make oven fries. Also, homemade burgers benefit hugely from the creative embellishments you'll find in Tasty Toppings for Plant-Based Burgers (page 143).

OPTIONS

For the beans, simply use your favorite variety, or whatever is in your pantry. These work especially well with pinto, red, and black beans but can be made with chickpeas and white beans, too.

FOR THE ONION AND GARLIC SAUTÉ

1 tablespoon extra-virgin olive oil

1 medium onion, finely chopped

2 to 3 cloves garlic, minced

FOR THE BASE

1 (15-ounce) can beans, drained and rinsed, or about 1½ cups cooked beans (see options at left)

1½ cups plant-based ground or crumbled tempeh

¾ cup quick-cooking oats

¾ cup fine bread crumbs

FOR THE FLAVOR BOMB

1 cup prepared salsa, barbecue sauce, marinara sauce, or Indian simmer sauce

1 tablespoon barbecue seasoning

Freshly ground pepper to taste

1 Preheat the oven to 350ºF. Line a roasting pan or baking sheet with parchment paper.

2 Heat the oil in a small skillet. Add the onion and sauté over medium heat until translucent. Add the garlic and continue to sauté until the onion is golden, 5 to 7 minutes.

3 Combine the onion mixture with the base ingredients in a food processor and pulse until evenly and finely chopped. Stop the machine to stir once or twice, scraping down the sides.

4 Spray the inside of a measuring cup—$\frac{1}{3}$ cup for small burgers, $\frac{1}{2}$ cup for large burgers—with cooking oil spray, or spread a little oil in the cup with a paper towel.

5 Scoop some of the bean mixture into the cup, leveling it off but not packing it in too tightly. Invert the cup onto the parchment paper with a sharp tap to release the mixture. Repeat until all the bean mixture is used.

6 Spray the bottom of the measuring cup with cooking spray and flatten each burger to about a $\frac{1}{2}$-inch thickness. Wipe the bottom of the cup and respray from time to time to prevent the mixture from sticking.

7 Bake the patties for 15 minutes, or until the bottom is golden, then carefully flip and bake for an additional 10 minutes. Avoid overbaking, or the burgers might become dry.

8 Remove from the oven and let stand for 5 minutes or so before serving.

SAVORY
SAUSAGE

MAKES 8 LINKS

WHILE THIS MAY LOOK like a relatively long list of ingredients, these DIY sausages are surprisingly easy to make. It's almost like baking a cake: the dry ingredients are combined with the wet ingredients, then baked. Except you wind up with savory sausages rather than a pastry.

Incorporating beans or tofu into the mix makes for a more tender, less rubbery texture than you would get from a purely gluten-based sausage. Once the sausages are cooked and cooled, they can be sliced and sautéed, cooked on a grill or grill pan, or incorporated into any recipe calling for plant-based sausage.

VARIATIONS

Substitute 2 teaspoons of rubbed sage for the Italian seasoning.

For a spicier effect, add 1 to 2 teaspoons dried hot red pepper flakes in addition to the sriracha.

FOR THE DRY MIXTURE

2 cups gluten flour (vital wheat gluten), or more if necessary

2 tablespoons nutritional yeast

1 teaspoon baking powder

2 tablespoons barbecue seasoning

1 tablespoon smoked paprika

1 tablespoon Italian seasoning

2 teaspoons onion powder

Generous sprinkling of freshly ground pepper

FOR THE WET MIXTURE

1 firmly packed cup cooked or canned (drained and rinsed) cannellini or great northern beans, or mashed tofu

¾ cup water

2 tablespoons maple or agave syrup

2 tablespoons extra-virgin olive oil

¼ cup good-quality natural ketchup

¼ cup soy sauce

2 to 3 teaspoons sriracha or other hot sauce, or more to taste

1 Preheat the oven to 350°F.

2 Combine the dry ingredients in a bowl and stir.

3 Combine the wet ingredients in a food processor and blend until smooth.

4 Pour the wet ingredients into the dry ingredients and stir at first with a spoon, then work together with your hands to form a soft dough. If the dough is too sticky, sprinkle in a bit more gluten flour.

5 Turn the dough out onto a floured board and knead for a minute or two, until smooth and sturdy. Place in a bowl, cover, and let stand for about 15 minutes.

6 Divide the dough into 8 equal parts using a sharp serrated knife. Form each part into a sausage shape. The dough is rather stubborn, but do the best you can—it will take on a more definite shape while it steams in the oven.

7 Wrap each sausage individually in a piece of foil and twist the ends together, to resemble a large Tootsie Roll. Make the wrapping a bit loose, because the sausages will expand as they bake.

8 Arrange the foil-wrapped sausages in a shallow casserole dish, then pour in about ½ inch of water. Cover the casserole dish with foil.

9 Bake for 1 hour. About halfway through, replenish the water if necessary.

10 When cool enough to handle, unwrap the sausages and use as needed. Store the rest in the refrigerator in an airtight container and use within a few days. These sausages also freeze well. Wrap each in plastic wrap or small plastic bags, then pack in an airtight container. Use within a month.

Shown in Italian-Style Sausage & Peppers, page 74

TEMPEH
BREAKFAST
SAUSAGE PATTIES

MAKES 8 SMALL
PATTIES

WITH ITS SLIGHTLY FERMENTED flavor and unique texture, tempeh is an ideal ingredient for making homemade sausage patties. For breakfast, simply layer one of these patties onto an English muffin that's been spread with vegan butter or mayo. Add a slice of vegan cheese, and you've got a high-protein breakfast. These can also be served as a protein-boosting side dish for lunch or dinner—they're quite flavorful even without any embellishment. Try these in Tofu and Bacon or Sausage Breakfast Muffins (page 196).

1 (8-ounce) package tempeh, any variety

½ cup quick-cooking oats

2 teaspoons dried onion flakes

1 teaspoon garlic granules

¼ cup good-quality natural ketchup

2 tablespoons maple or agave syrup

1 tablespoon barbecue seasoning

1 to 2 teaspoons sriracha or other hot
    sauce (optional)

2 teaspoons Italian seasoning

2 teaspoons smoked paprika

1 tablespoon extra-virgin olive oil

2 tablespoons water

Cooking oil spray (optional)

Safflower or other high-heat oil for
    frying (optional)

1 Break up the tempeh into several pieces and combine it in a food processor with the oats, onion flakes, garlic granules, ketchup, maple syrup, barbecue seasoning, sriracha (if desired), Italian seasoning, paprika, olive oil, and water. Pulse until the tempeh is finely and evenly chopped; don't puree!

2 To fry: Spray the inside of a ¼ cup measure with cooking oil spray, or spread a little oil in the cup with a paper towel.

3 Scoop some of the tempeh mixture into the cup, leveling it off but not packing it in too tightly. Invert the cup onto a flat surface and release the mixture with a sharp tap. Repeat until all the mixture is used.

4 Spray the bottom of the measuring cup with cooking spray and flatten each patty to about a ½-inch thickness. Wipe the bottom of the cup and respray from time to time to prevent the mixture from sticking.

5 Heat just enough safflower oil to coat the bottom of a nonstick skillet over medium-low heat. Arrange the patties in the pan in a single layer (in batches if necessary) and fry on both sides until golden and crisp. Place on paper towel–lined plates to absorb extra oil, if desired.

6 **To bake:** Preheat the oven to 350°F. Line a baking sheet with parchment paper. Drop the tempeh mixture by the ¼ cup onto the prepared baking sheet. Flatten gently with the back of the cup. For a crisp texture, spray the patties with cooking oil spray, if desired, before placing in the oven. Bake for 15 minutes, then flip and bake for 15 minutes longer, or until both sides are golden brown.

CHAPTER 10
EXTRAS:
MARINADES,
SAUCES
& DRESSINGS

THIS FINAL CHAPTER PRESENTS some of the sauces and dressings used throughout the previous pages. If you've read this far, you've learned that I'm a big fan of shortcuts, especially now that most any supermarket offers a veritable cornucopia of ready-made sauces and other preparations that cut cooking time and save energy. I've also found that the shorter an ingredients list, the more likely that a busy cook (especially one new to plant-based fare) will want to make it.

For a long time, I just didn't love any of the bottled barbecue sauces I tried, so I made my own. Sodium content can be an issue with some bottled sauces, and many of them include high-fructose corn syrup. These are good reasons to have some easy DIY options if you can't find just what you want in bottled sauces in terms of flavor, nutrition, and price.

There are nights when I want to just open a bottle of all-natural peanut satay sauce, for example, and other times when it doesn't seem like a big deal to make the homemade kind, which can't be beat for its luscious flavor (though it makes an additional sticky dish to wash). Options are always welcome, and that's why this chapter is here.

COCONUT PEANUT SAUCE

HERE'S A PERFECT EXAMPLE of a sauce that comes in really decent bottled versions but that is just so much better when you make it yourself. Many of the bottled sauces I've tried have great flavor, and I do tend to keep this kind of sauce—usually called peanut satay sauce—as a pantry staple. But it's the lush texture of coconut milk and peanut butter in this homemade version that the bottled kind can't quite match. The latter is very good, but this recipe is next-level yum.

⅔ cup natural crunchy or smooth peanut butter, at room temperature

¾ cup light coconut milk

2 tablespoons reduced-sodium soy sauce, or to taste

2 teaspoons grated fresh or squeeze-bottle ginger

½ teaspoon sriracha or other hot sauce, plus more for serving

2 tablespoons natural granulated sugar or coconut sugar

Juice of ½ to 1 lime, to taste

1 Combine all ingredients in a small mixing bowl and whisk until completely blended.

2 Store leftovers in a tightly covered container in the refrigerator for up to four days.

JERK SAUCE

JERK SAUCE IS ONE of the few sauces for which I haven't found a bottled equivalent that I love—the predominant flavor is usually salt. I'll be the first to admit that my interpretation isn't quite authentic, but it does have the right flavor notes—sweet, savory, citrusy, and spicy. You can cook almost any kind of plant protein in this sauce, and it's completely transformed.

Use this sauce as directed in recipes; it needs to be cooked briefly in order to thicken.

1 tablespoon cornstarch or arrowroot

2 tablespoons water

⅔ cup orange juice

2 tablespoons molasses, maple syrup, or agave syrup

2 tablespoons soy sauce

Juice of 1 lime

1 small hot chili pepper, seeded and minced, or ½ teaspoon dried hot red pepper flakes

1 tablespoon Jamaican jerk seasoning

1 Dissolve the cornstarch in the water in a small bowl. Add the remaining ingredients and stir.

2 Leftovers can be stored in a tightly covered container or small jar and will keep in the refrigerator for up to four days.

Shown in Jamaican Jerk Skillet or Bowls, page 57

VEGAN RANCH DRESSING

MAKES ABOUT 1½ CUPS

MANY, IF NOT MOST, dressings are already vegan or come in vegan versions. Ranch is one of the few that isn't easy to find dairy-free, so here's an easy one to whip up using white beans as a creamy base.

¾ cup canned cannellini or great northern beans, drained and rinsed

¼ cup plain unsweetened plant-based milk or water

¼ cup vegan mayonnaise

2 tablespoons freshly squeezed lemon juice

1 tablespoon apple cider vinegar

1 teaspoon salt-free seasoning

½ teaspoon dried dill

½ teaspoon dried onion flakes or garlic granules

Freshly ground pepper to taste

1 Combine all ingredients in a food processor or blender. Process until completely smooth.

2 Transfer to a tightly sealed bottle or a container with a pour spout and store in the refrigerator for up to a week.

Shown in Buffalo Chick'n Salad, page 174

TARTAR SAUCE
OR DRESSING

MAKES ABOUT 3/4 CUP

THIS VEGAN VERSION OF a classic cold sauce is almost silly-easy. It's my favorite condiment for vegan burgers (with or without buns), and it makes a flavorful spread for wraps. It's also particularly good with plant-based seafood.

Whatever is left over also makes a tasty dip for raw vegetables such as bell peppers, carrots, celery, and broccoli.

⅔ cup vegan mayonnaise

1 tablespoon sweet pickle relish

1 tablespoon prepared yellow mustard

1 Combine all ingredients in a small bowl and stir until well blended.

2 Store leftovers in a tightly covered container in the refrigerator for up to four days.

QUICK NO-COOK BARBECUE SAUCE

MAKES ABOUT 2 CUPS

ONE UPON A TIME, there weren't many good natural barbecue sauces available in grocery stores. They were too salty, too smoky, or in some other way weren't just right. Today there are several good choices, but I still seem to be in the habit of making my own. This one uses pantry staples I almost always have on hand and takes only a couple of minutes to make. But as with any kind of sauce, the choice is yours: if you have a favorite bottled sauce, go for it!

This yields a plentiful amount, more than you'll need for a typical recipe. Trust me—you'll use it up. And if you see that it hasn't disappeared within three or four days in the fridge, pack it into a container and freeze it until the next time you need it.

1 (15-ounce) can tomato sauce

¼ cup maple or agave syrup

2 tablespoons apple cider vinegar

2 tablespoons soy sauce

1 tablespoon barbecue seasoning blend

2 teaspoons sweet or smoked paprika

Freshly ground pepper

1 Combine all ingredients in a mixing bowl and stir.

2 If time allows, cover and let stand for 30 minutes or longer to allow the flavors to blend. But if you need to use the dressing right away, go ahead—it'll still be quite good.

3 Store leftovers in a tightly covered container in the refrigerator for up to a week.

TERIYAKI SAUCE

MAKES ABOUT
3/4 CUP

I THINK HOMEMADE AND bottled teriyaki sauce are about equal when it comes to flavor. It comes down to whether the ingredients are staples in your kitchen. If not, it might make sense to use a good bottled sauce. Still, this recipe is handy to have in case you're in midrecipe and realize you need teriyaki sauce—it only takes a couple of minutes to whip up.

¼ cup soy sauce

2 teaspoons dark sesame oil

3 tablespoons agave syrup

¼ cup white wine vinegar or rice vinegar

2 teaspoons grated fresh or squeeze-bottle ginger (optional)

2 teaspoons sesame seeds (optional)

1 Combine all ingredients in a bottle. Seal tightly and shake before using.

2 Store leftovers in a tightly covered container in the refrigerator for a week or longer.

SIMPLE
SALSA FRESCA

**MAKES ABOUT
2½ CUPS**

WHEN TOMATOES ARE AT their best, it's a treat to make fresh salsa at home. You'll find salsa called for throughout this book, and though I don't necessarily refer to this recipe in particular, it's well worth considering during the summer months. And of course it's fantastic when served with chips alongside many of the dishes in chapter 6 (page 147). This is best to make when you know it will be used right away.

VARIATIONS

Chipotle: Substitute 1 or 2 canned chipotle chilies in adobo for the fresh hot peppers and process as directed.

Fresh corn: Stir in the kernels from a lightly boiled or grilled ear of corn after processing.

Peach, nectarine, mango, or apricot: Add between ½ cup and 1 cup peeled, pitted, and coarsely chopped fresh fruit to the other ingredients and process as directed.

2 cups diced ripe fresh tomatoes

¼ cup finely chopped red onion

1 clove garlic, minced (optional)

1 or 2 jalapeño peppers, seeded and coarsely chopped

¼ cup chopped fresh cilantro or parsley

Juice of ½ to 1 lemon or lime

¼ teaspoon salt

1 Combine all ingredients in a food processor and pulse until the mixture becomes a coarse puree. Transfer to a shallow serving bowl and serve.

2 Store leftovers in a tightly covered container in the refrigerator for a day or two.

EASY
PLANT PARMESAN

MAKES ¾ CUP

NOWADAYS, THERE ARE SUPER-HARD vegan Parmesan cheeses available in the supermarket, just waiting for your grater. They're amazingly easy to work with, unlike the dry, crumbly animal-based kind. But if you find the vegan product too pricey—or if you can't find it at all—you'll appreciate this recipe.

There's no easier plant-based Parmesan than this! Start with blanched slivered almonds, grind them down, then add nutritional yeast and salt. Or easier still—start with almond flour. You won't even need a machine.

A tablespoon or two of nutritional yeast gives you your daily dose of vitamin B_{12}, a valuable nutrient in a plant-based diet. Almond flour is also a great source of vitamin E and calcium.

This makes a tasty topping for many of the pasta dishes in chapter 3 (page 61), and it's excellent as a topping for soups and stews.

¾ cup blanched slivered almonds
  or ½ cup almond flour

¼ cup nutritional yeast

¼ teaspoon salt

1 If using slivered almonds, pulse them in a food processor until finely ground.

2 Combine all ingredients in a small bowl and stir thoroughly.

3 Store in a tightly covered container in the refrigerator for up to several weeks.

VERY GREEN PESTO

MAKES ABOUT 1 CUP

STRETCH YOUR PESTO BY using baby greens in conjunction with the requisite basil or parsley. Not only will the mixture stay greener; it will also cover more pasta and go further in other dishes. It makes a great sandwich spread in place of the usual condiments, too. Try it with Big Roast Beefy Sandwiches (page 130), for example. You can toss it with pasta and top with your favorite kind of prepared meatballs or homemade Plant-Powered Meatballs (page 227). And it's fantastic as a topping for Italian-style soups, such as Sausage, Potato, and Escarole Soup (page 4).

NOTE: *Garlic will make this pesto tastier, though some of us—yours truly included—don't like it raw. You can mince and sauté it first in the olive oil designated for the pesto to temper its bite.*

1 tablespoon extra-virgin olive oil

1 to 2 cloves garlic, crushed (optional; see note)

Juice of ½ lemon, or more to taste

½ cup chopped walnuts

5 ounces baby spinach, arugula, and/or power greens (see page 56)

½ cup firmly packed fresh basil or parsley leaves

Pinch of salt

Freshly ground pepper to taste

1 Combine the olive oil, garlic (if using), lemon juice, walnuts, spinach, and basil in a food processor and pulse until the mixture becomes a coarse, even puree. You may need to add the greens in batches if your processor has a small or medium-size container. Stop the machine from time to time to scrape down the sides. You may need to add a tablespoon or two of water to keep the mixture flowing.

2 Once the mixture reaches the desired consistency, add more lemon juice if desired, season gently with salt and pepper, then pulse a few more times. Transfer to a small bowl and serve at the table or use as directed in recipes.

3 Store leftovers in a tightly covered container in the refrigerator for a day or two.

MUSHROOM
GRAVY / WITH AN ONION VARIATION

MAKES ABOUT 2 CUPS

A BOOK ABOUT MEATY plant proteins wouldn't be complete without a recipe for a great, easy vegan gravy. And while I don't call for it often, feel free to use it on any simply prepared plant protein. It's especially good with Chicken-Style Seitan Cutlets (page 222) and Classic Meat Loaf (page 30), particularly if you choose to omit the tomatoey topping from the latter.

For a simple main dish, cut any type of plant protein (including tofu, tempeh, and seitan) into strips. Sauté in a little olive oil until golden on most sides. Top potatoes (baked and smashed) with the protein, then smother with this gravy. Serve with a salad for an easy and satisfying dinner.

VARIATION

Quarter and thinly slice a large onion or two medium onions. Cook slowly in a skillet with a little olive oil (about a tablespoon would do) until golden or lightly browned, as you prefer. Add to the gravy after it thickens.

2 cups vegetable broth

6 to 8 ounces cremini (baby bella) or white mushrooms, cleaned, stemmed, and sliced

2 tablespoons soy sauce

3 tablespoons cornstarch or arrowroot

Pinch of dried thyme, basil, or Italian seasoning (optional)

2 tablespoons nutritional yeast (optional but highly recommended)

1 Combine the broth, mushrooms, and soy sauce in a small saucepan and bring to a slow boil. Reduce the heat and simmer until the mushrooms are wilted, about 5 minutes.

2 Meanwhile, combine the cornstarch with just enough water to make it smooth and pourable.

3 Slowly whisk the dissolved cornstarch into the simmering broth, stirring constantly with a whisk until the mixture is thickened.

4 Remove from the heat and stir in the dried herbs and nutritional yeast, if desired. Use at once or cover and keep warm until needed. Store leftovers in a tightly covered container in the refrigerator for three days.

RECIPES BY

PROTEIN
TYPE

This index will allow you to quickly locate recipes for the type of protein you may have on hand or want to try. For example, let's say you have a package of vegan sausages and want to find all the recipes in this book that might call for them: just scan to find those options.

Recipes calling for classic plant proteins—tofu, tempeh, and seitan— as well as some of the DIY meaty proteins are incorporated into this list. Recipes offering the option of using seitan would be found under "Beefy Chunks or Strips"; tempeh is more likely to be used in recipes calling for beefy ground, and tofu is primarily used in chicken-style recipes. You can also consult the general index (page 256) to find recipes in which tofu, tempeh, and seitan are suggested as options in addition to the prepared plant-based meats.

You may see some recipes listed twice in this index, which will be the case if a recipe is flexible in terms of the style of protein used or if more than one type of protein is called for in a single recipe.

Mom's "Tuna"-Noodle
Casserole, page 42

PLANT-BASED
PROTEIN OPTIONS & BRANDS

Here's a rundown of some of the major players in the plant-protein field. This landscape is changing and growing rapidly. New companies are popping up all the time, while small companies are being bought by large ones.

There are a number of plant-protein companies you may be familiar with—such as MorningStar Farms and Quorn—whose products aren't vegan; that is, they include eggs and/or dairy products. It's quite likely that they'll be developing some all-vegan products in order to compete in this marketplace.

If you're interested in a particular brand, make sure to go to the company's website and search for the store locator to learn whether you can find its products in your area. If not, there are some excellent online markets that sell them, such as VeganEssentials.com, VeganSupplyCo.com, FakeMeats.com, and, of course, the online elephant in the room—Amazon.com. A small number of the companies listed in this section take online orders as well.

Many supermarket chains are developing their own proprietary store brands of plant-based meat alternatives. Aldi and Trader Joe's offer quite a nice array of products, for example, and other chains are jumping into this sector as well. It would be daunting to list all the store chains' offerings here, so instead the focus is on independent companies and their products.

While the following appendix lists U.S. and Canadian companies, it's important to note the growing number of European companies producing plant-based meats. Just a few are Oumph (Sweden), the Meatless Farm Company (U.K.), Vivera (Netherlands), and Foods of Tomorrow (Spain). There are many others, and as in North America, more are coming on board all the time. In addition, companies like Impossible foods are making inroads in Europe and other global markets. The coming years are sure to give us an expanding array of global plant-based meat options!

If you're interested in complete nutrition information and ingredients lists for any of these products, you can always look them up on the company website. Here, just the primary protein sources are given.

ABBOT'S BUTCHER Protein sources: Soy-free, gluten-free, non-GMO pea protein

Slow-Roast Chopped "Chicken"

Spanish Smoked "Chorizo"

Umami Ground "Beef"

AMY'S Amy's product line includes many ready-to-eat meals, but they've expanded their line of what they call Veggie Meats. Primary protein sources vary from one product to the next. Some include tofu, lentils, soybeans, quinoa, rice, bulgur, and wheat gluten.

Burgers (several varieties, including Organic California Veggie Burger, All American Veggie Burger, Black Bean Veggie Burger)

Veggie Meatballs

Meatless Veggie Sausages

BEYOND MEAT Protein sources: Pea, mung bean, fava bean, rice, and sunflower seed proteins

Beyond Burger

Beyond Beef Plant-Based Ground

Beyond Sausage Brat Original

Beyond Sausage Hot Italian

Beyond Beef Crumbles

BUTLER Protein source: Non-GMO whole soybeans

Soy Curls

DR. PRAEGER'S Note that not all of this company's products are vegan. For example, the products labeled as fish really are fish. Listed below are their "Pure Plant Protein" products, which use pea protein as the primary protein source.

Classic Chick'n Tenders

Perfect Burger

Sunday Funday Veggie Sausages

FIELD ROAST Protein source: Vital wheat gluten

Sausages (several varieties)

Deli Slices (several varieties)

Holiday Roasts and Loaves (several varieties)

Hand-Formed FieldBurger

Wings

Cutlets

Frankfurters

GARDEIN Gardein makes a wide array of meat alternatives, and the primary protein source varies among products. Sources include pea protein concentrate, soy protein isolate, soy protein concentrate, vital wheat gluten, and ancient grain flour.

Burgers and Sliders (several varieties)

Chick'n (several varieties)

Turk'y Cutlet

Golden Fishless Filet

Mini Crispy Crabless Cakes

Beefless (several varieties, including ground, tips, and strips)

Spicy Breakfast Saus'age Patties

Sliced Italian Saus'age

GOOD CATCH Protein sources: Six-plant protein blend (pea protein isolate, soy protein concentrate, chickpea flour, lentil protein, faba protein, navy bean flour)

Fish-Free Tuna (several varieties)

Plant-Based Crab Cakes

Plant-Based Fish Burgers

Plant-Based Fish Cakes

LIGHTLIFE Protein sources vary.

Burgers (pea protein)

Smart Dogs, Jumbo Smart Dogs, and Tofu Pups (soy protein isolate)

Smart Bacon (soy protein isolate and vital wheat gluten)

Smoky Tempeh Strips (also known as Fakin' Bacon; cultured organic soybeans)

Tempeh (four varieties; organic soybeans, grains, and seeds)

LOMA LINDA Protein sources: Soy protein concentrate, textured vegetable protein

Taco Filling

Tuno (several varieties)

Vegetable Skallops

LONGEVE Protein source: Pea protein

Plant-Based Protein Crumbles (several varieties)

MAIKA Protein source: Soy-free, gluten-free pea protein

Veggie Burger

Veggie Dog

Veggie Steak

MORNINGSTAR FARMS Protein sources vary. Note that a few of this company's products contain egg whites, but far fewer than in the past. Check labels!

Vegan Burgers (several varieties, including beans, vegetables, seeds, grains, wheat gluten, and/ or soy protein isolate)

Veggie Meal Starters Chik'n Strips (several varieties, including soy protein isolate, wheat gluten, soy protein concentrate, black beans, and/or soy flour)

Veggie Meal Starters Chipotle Black Bean Crumbles (soy protein concentrate, black beans)

Veggie Meal Starters Chorizo Crumbles (soy flour)

Veggie Meal Starters Grillers Crumbles (soy flour)

NASOYA Protein source: Organic soybeans

Organic Tofu (several varieties, including firm, extra firm, sprouted super firm, cubed super firm, and silken)

TofuBaked (several varieties)

NO EVIL FOODS Protein sources: Non-GMO vital wheat gluten, chickpea flour

Comrade Cluck "No Chicken"

El Zapatista "Chorizo"

The Stallion "Italian Sausage" (includes red kidney beans)

Pit Boss "Pulled 'Pork'" Barbecue

The Pardon "Holiday Centerpiece" (includes white beans)

NUGGS Protein sources: Soy and what protein

Crispy chicken-style nuggets

SOPHIE'S KITCHEN Protein sources vary and include brown rice flakes and pea protein.

Breaded shrimp

Toona (several varieties)

Smoked Salmon

SOYBOY Protein source: Organic tofu

Tofu (firm and extra firm)

Tempeh

Baked Tofu (several varieties)

Veggie Bacon

Not Dogs (includes isolated soy protein)

SWEET EARTH FOODS Protein sources (in various combinations, depending on product): Vital wheat gluten, soybeans, soy protein concentrate.

Burgers (many varieties)

Grounds (several varieties)

Benevolent Bacon

Harmless Ham Deli Slices

Mindful Chick'n

Seitan (many varieties)

TOFURKY Protein sources: Vital wheat gluten and/or organic tofu unless otherwise indicated

Deli Slices (several varieties)

Roasts

Chick'n (several varieties)

Plant-Based Crumbles (includes soy flour)

Sausages and Hot Dogs (several varieties)

Treehouse Tempeh (several varieties, including marinated strips; includes organic soybeans)

UPTON'S NATURALS Upton's is a major producer of jackfruit products, though these are not a significant source of protein. The protein source in their seitan products is vital wheat gluten.

Seitan (several varieties)

THE VERY GOOD BUTCHERS All products list wheat gluten as a primary ingredient; red beans, adzuki beans, and barley are listed in various products as well.

Pepperoni

Roast Beast

Smokin' Bangers

Smokin' Burgers

Taco Stuffer

Ribz

VIANA Protein sources: Tofu, organic wheat protein

Cowgirl Veggie Steaks

Veggie Chickin Nuggets

Veggie Gyros (beefy strips)

WESTSOY Protein sources: For tofu and tempeh, organic soybeans; for seitan, vital wheat gluten

Tofu (several varieties)

Baked tofu (several varieties)

Tempeh (several varieties)

Seitan (several varieties)

YVES VEGGIE CUISINE Protein sources vary.

Veggie Dogs (several varieties, including soy protein isolate, vital wheat gluten, tofu)

Veggie Bacon (vital wheat gluten, soy protein isolate)

Veggie Ground Round (textured soy protein concentrate)

Deli slices (several varieties, including vital wheat gluten, tofu; some varieties contain soy protein isolate)

HONORABLE MENTION: THE JACKFRUIT COMPANY Even though jackfruit isn't a good source of protein, I list it here because it has gotten to be a popular meat alternative. In a couple of recipes in this book, I've suggested combining jackfruit with another plant protein source. The main ingredient in the Jackfruit Company's products is, not surprisingly, jackfruit. Meal starters come in several varieties, including Barbecue, Lightly Seasoned, and Teriyaki.

SOURCES

Caroline Bushnell, "Newly Released Market Data Shows Soaring Demand for Plant-Based Food" (Good Food Institute, September 12, 2018).

Jennifer Grebow, "Pea Protein Market Will Not Be as Big as Soy, but Will Offer Unique Benefits as a Specialty Protein, Says Pea Supplier" (*Nutritional Outlook*, July 20, 2018).

Matthew Kadey, "Is Soy Bad for You?" (*Runner's World*, June 7, 2019).

Ron Milo, "Scrap the Meat: Might Plants Be the Key to Food Security?" (*Weizmann Compass*, May 1, 2018).

Daniel Pendick, "How Much Protein Do You Need Every Day?" (*Harvard Health Blog*, June 25, 2015).

Nathaniel Popper, "This Animal Activist Used to Get in Your Face. Now He's Going After Your Palate" (*New York Times*, March 12, 2019).

"Rearing Cattle Produces More Greenhouse Gases Than Driving Cars, UN Report Warns" (*UN News*, November 29, 2006).

Michael Pellman Rowland, "Millennials Are Driving the Worldwide Shift Away from Meat" (*Forbes*, March 23, 2018).

US Department of Health and Human Services, Office of Disease Prevention and Health Promotion, "Nutritional Goals for Age-Sex Groups Based on Dietary Reference Intakes and *Dietary Guidelines* Recommendations," Dietary Guidelines 2015–2020, appendix 7, table A7-1.

IMPERIAL TO METRIC CONVERSIONS

VOLUME MEASUREMENT CONVERSIONS

Cups	Tablespoons	Teaspoons	Milliliters
		1 tsp	5 ml
1⁄16 cup	1 tbsp	3 tsp	15 ml
1⁄8 cup	2 tbsp	6 tsp	30 ml
1⁄4 cup	4 tbsp	12 tsp	60 ml
1⁄3 cup	5 1⁄3 tbsp	16 tsp	80 ml
1⁄2 cup	8 tbsp	24 tsp	120 ml
2⁄3 cup	10 2⁄3 tbsp	32 tsp	160 ml
3⁄4 cup	12 tbsp	36 tsp	180 ml
1 cup	16 tbsp	48 tsp	240 ml

WEIGHT MEASUREMENT CONVERSIONS

US	Metric
1 ounce	28.4 grams (g)
8 ounces	227 grams
16 ounces (1 pound)	454 grams

COOKING TEMPERATURE CONVERSIONS

Celsius/Centigrade	$F = (C \times 1.8) + 32$
Fahrenheit	$C = (F - 32) \times 0.5556$

INDEX

ACKNOWLEDGMENTS

I've never been one for long, gushy acknowledgments, so keeping to my personal tradition, I'll keep this set short and sweet as well. I'd like to give a shout-out to:

Morgan Hedden, my editor, who saw the potential in this project and gave me the leeway to run with it.

Sally Ekus and Lisa Ekus, my agents and dear friends.

Hannah Kaminsky, talented food photographer and longtime collaborator.

Barbara Clark, for her granular copy-editing skills.

The editorial team at Grand Central Publishing, whose enthusiasm for this project has been the icing on the (vegan) cake.

Laura Palese, whose handsome page design pulls all the elements together.

My immediate and extended family and friends, ever willing to be my taste-testers.

And to the entrepreneurs behind the plant-based protein companies, thank you for what you do for the planet and the animals.

MY MOST SINCERE THANKS TO ALL!

ABOUT THE AUTHOR

NAVA ATLAS is the author of many bestselling vegetarian and vegan cookbooks, including *5-Ingredient Vegan, Vegan on a Budget, Wild About Greens, Vegan Holiday Kitchen,* and *Vegan Soups and Hearty Stews for All Seasons.* Nava also creates visual books on women's issues and runs two websites, The Vegan Atlas (theveganatlas.com) and Literary Ladies Guide (literaryladiesguide.com). She lives in the Hudson Valley region of New York State with her family.